1000 ideas for English Term Papers

ROBERT A. FARMER

ARCO PUBLISHING COMPANY, INC.

219 Park Avenue South, New York, N.Y. 10003

Sixth Printing, 1978

An Arc Book
Published by Arco Publishing Company, Inc.
219 Park Avenue South, New York, N.Y. 10003

Copyright © 1967 by Robert A. Farmer

Library of Congress Catalog Card Number 67-11921
ISBN 0-668-01548-9

Printed in the United States of America

Contents

Preface

ALTHOUGH term paper time may be the high point of the school year academically, it often proves to be the low point for student morale. Yet there is no good reason why writing a term paper should be any more difficult than other assignments. In composing a term paper, the student is given the freedom to pursue his individual interests to a much greater extent than in other aspects of his study. For this reason, one would think that this task would be anticipated with pleasure rather than dread. Yet it is this very chance for independence that produces all the panic as the deadline date draws near.

This book is designed to eliminate some of the anxieties that arise as the hesitant author or critic grapples with his assignment. I have tried to approach the task of writing a paper strictly from the point of view of the student (the average literate student, not the nascent Hemingway) and have assembled some of the more useful techniques for decreasing wasted effort and increasing averages. While the collection of hints does not presume to replace the standard works on grammar and form, I hope that it will prove a practical and unpedantic guide through some of the difficulties of the term paper's gestation period.

The compilation of topics that comprises the bulk of the book may be more immediately helpful to the harried student than the text. I have gathered what I hope to be a representative and stimulating assortment, to demonstrate the wealth of approaches that a student can make to the subject matter.

For their invaluable assistance in compiling the topics, and for their many ideas on the ingredients of a good paper, I am very grateful to my student contributors: Alfred Bartlett, Gene Kirkam, Anthony Day, and Lowry Pei, of Harvard; Kay King, of Wellesley; and Linda Fowler, of Smith.

—ROBERT A. FARMER

PART I

A SHORT GUIDE TO THE ART OF TERM PAPER WRITING

CHAPTER 1

Introduction

WRITING an English paper is never easy. From the time you begin to work on it to that relieved but hesitant moment when you lay your offering on the teacher's desk, it sometimes seems as if you are wringing each word from a spongelike mind, which has already been squeezed dry. No one should expect the words to flow from his pen in a creative torrent, although many students waste valuable time waiting for this miracle to happen. Writing almost always involves more concentration than inspiration, and this is particularly true of writing term papers.

While producing a manuscript of any length is always hard work, it is not necessarily a corollary truth that a good paper is harder to write than a mediocre one. While more preparation may be required, and all aspects must necessarily be handled with greater precision, on the whole, many of the techniques that make a paper successful will also result in a reduction of wasted time and effort. In addition, the satisfaction—even the excitement—of knowing that you are turning out something worthwhile is bound to make the task far less of a burden for you.

So, as long as you have to write a paper anyway, why not write a good one?

A good term paper has a point to make, which it states clearly and concisely. It displays sound organization and effective use of language. Ideally, it teaches something to both writer and reader.

The first section of this book briefly discusses the necessary elements of a sound paper, from concept to completion. It should help you to develop an efficient and logical method of working with your ideas and start you thinking creatively about your project.

The second section offers an extensive list of term-paper topics to which you can apply these ideas. They should help you to formulate an interesting topic for your particular assignment.

As something like an idea or an approach begins to grow in your mind, start working with it immediately. A term paper does not spring forth full blown from the writer's imagination. It must be coaxed every step of the way. Work is the prime requisite of a good paper, and so if you know that you are not going to put much effort into the assignment, at least be honest with yourself: choose a topic of modest scope and do it competently. If achieving a higher grade and meeting an intellectual challenge have any meaning for you, try to make a realistic evaluation of your goals and of what it will take to reach them.

We are not about to preach to you on why and how you should write the perfect term paper. We *will* try to give you some suggestions to help you do as good a job as you want to do.

CHAPTER 2

The Search for a Topic

CHOOSING a topic to write about is the key step in the process of composing a research paper. The topic you select will not only have a great effect upon the amount of time you need for the research, organization, and writing, it may also determine the quality of the finished paper. A few hours of preliminary planning will save many hours of panic later on, if you follow a few simple rules. Perhaps the simplest of these to state and the most difficult to apply is: learn self-discipline. Especially in the early stages of work on a paper, it is invaluable. To those who abhor the idea of organizing their thoughts, may we suggest that the exercise of self-control in the choice of a topic will permit the luxury of procrastination later on.

A number of considerations, both intellectual and practical, come into play in the search for a topic. The first step may be to choose the *material* that your paper will discuss. This can be a particular work, a favorite author, a literary form (such as the epic poem), or a literary movement. Perhaps, on the other hand, you may decide to let the subject be determined by the approach you select. If you have been assigned specific material to work with, of course, then this is not a problem.

Second, decide on the *approach* that best suits your interests and skills. There are at least six ways of approaching any subject. Consider the following: *biographical, historical, textual, stylis-*

tic, thematic, and *comparative.* These approaches are normally found in combination, but starting with only one may breed an idea.

Suppose that you have been assigned William Faulkner's *The Sound and the Fury.* Here are some of the directions that each of the six approaches might suggest:

(1) Biographical

Scope: The role of the book in Faulkner's development as a writer.

Approach: Compare with earlier and later works for differences in style and attitude. Is this book in any way a culmination or a beginning of a trend?

(2) Historical

Scope: The effect of southern life on the book.

Approach: Could the same story have been set in another region?

(3) Textual

Scope: Examination of narrative structure.

Approach: Is there an order to the revelation of events and of the characters' points of view? What is its over-all effect?

(4) Stylistic

Scope: What is the source of the book's impact?

Approach: Rewrite several paragraphs in your own words. How does Faulkner's use of the language differ from yours? How is his more powerful?

(5) Thematic

Scope: Someone has said, "Every story boils down to one paragraph." Is this true of The Sound and The Fury? *If so, does it fit into one of the main themes which run through Faulkner's work?*

(6) Comparative

Scope: Faulkner states, "Dilsey is one of my own favorite characters, because she is brave, courageous, generous, gentle, and honest." How does she differ from other characters whom Faulkner created?

As your third consideration, determine the *breadth of your topic,* seeking to avoid the pitfalls of superficiality and of meaningless detail. Carefully consider *your* involvement with the subject in terms of interest and time.

Finally, *evaluate* the topic in its relationship to the course for which it was assigned.

If you have done all these things with reasonable honesty, you are ready for a brief check of the research facilities available to you. Don't hesitate to change your mind if the information seems scarce or out of date. The time you lose at this point is insignificant in comparison with what you might waste in a last-minute search for nonexistent data. Frequently, in such instances, your original idea for a topic need not be abandoned, but only revised.

Good topics can be the product of creativity, curiosity, or frustration, but they all have several characteristics in common. In varying degrees, a topic should reflect *you* (by displaying a realistic awareness of your intellectual level and expectations) ; it should have a broad enough appeal to be of interest to your teacher, who after reading twenty-nine other papers, might appreciate your thoughtfulness; and it should appear to have some purpose other than that of merely satisfying an academic requirement. Although it is natural that you should want to choose a topic that is both interesting and profitable to you, it frequently happens that papers are assigned for subjects that do not fire your enthusiasm. In such circumstances, it is wise to relate other courses which *do* stimulate you to the one for which you are writing. For example: you might discuss various historical events in relation to certain literary movements, such as the Restoration Period; the influence of artistic styles on literary imagery and symbols as seen in the work of Hogarth and Fielding; or the effect of scientific terminology and methods on poetic expréssion. This interdisciplinary approach gives your topic an aura of originality, supplies you with valuable background for other courses, and widens the scope of materials available for research.

Choose your topic to complement your skills as a writer and thinker. More important, do *not* choose one that will overemphasize your intellectual weaknesses. If you have a rather prosaic mind, avoid poetic analysis, since you may not be capable of appreciating the subtleties of imagery and tone that distinguish the poet's work. Similarly, don't be entrapped by whimsical or "gimmicky" topics, unless you have the flair to handle them successfully. If inspiration seems to fail you, your wisest course will be to aim for a topic that you can handle competently.

Such a topic is one on which you can use organization, thoroughness, and careful style as a substitute when real creativity is lacking. Such a topic usually involves strict comparison or close analysis of a narrowly defined topic. With only a small area of material to be covered, it can—and must —be treated well. A short but crucial scene of a play may reveal much about the structure and theme of the play as a whole and serve as an important link in the actions that lead to the climax.

This type of topic will also sharpen your perception and widen your understanding of the entire work. A single speech or passage of description from a novel may display character development or the author's point of view or may be a good example of the author's literary style. In any case, such a topic should have potential for examples, which can be used to fortify your points and lend weight to your arguments.

Your topic should have certain limits, imposed partly by you and partly by the nature of the subject matter. Your definition of the topic will affect the entire procedure of research, organization, and composition. The problem of definition can best be understood by examining the effect that a too-narrow or too-broad topic can have upon a paper.

Most students either overestimate their capabilities or underestimate the subject. A realistic attitude toward the length and quality of the paper that you wish to produce will spare you a great deal of dismay the day before it is due. Don't hesitate to consider your interest in the course and the amount of time you are willing to spend doing research as factors in the type of topic you chose. If your ambitions are limited, don't involve yourself in discussions of obscure symbolism or in making theories about an author's purpose. You will undoubtedly be exhausted before your subject is, and, what is worse, you will wind up with bits of unrelated information, which are difficult to rework or to put together into an intelligible whole.

Even more treacherous than an overambitious topic is one that lacks direction and boundaries. Researching this sort of topic will lead you everywhere and nowhere, and your notes will be a discouraging jumble. Such a paper will give the impression that you didn't read anything at all. Examples of "directionless" topics might be "Wordsworth's Use of Nature," or "Dostoevski's Attitude Toward Religion." Such topics can be made quite workable, however, by the introduction of specific references.

Treating only one or a limited number of an author's works is a basic way of limiting a topic, but a more sophisticated method is one that incorporates an approach. Thus, "Wordsworth's Use of Nature" becomes "Nature as a Muse in [the poet's] 'Intimations of Immortality' " and implies a stylistic approach. "Dostoevski's Attitude Toward Religion" becomes "Prince Mishkin as a Christ Figure in *The Idiot*," suggesting a semi-biographical and thematic approach.

When choosing a topic or developing an approach to a subject, keep in view the nature of the course for which the paper was assigned. Try to think of your paper as a learning process rather than as a collection of facts. You should also attempt to discern the motives that lay behind the assignment; in other words, determine what skills or points of view your teacher wants you to acquire in writing the paper. It may have been intended primarily as an exercise in organization and logical presentation, in which case a relatively simple and straightforward topic will be most suitable. A paper may also be assigned to introduce breadth or depth into a sketchy survey course. In this instance, your wisest choice of subject will be an author or a literary period that has been omitted from the syllabus because of limited time, or one that was discussed only briefly. An alternative would be to choose a common theme or image and treat it in such a manner as to unify the various elements of the course.

You may find it very helpful to review your class notes to find clues to the type of approach that your teacher has in mind. Lecture notes are also useful, as they highlight the most important areas of the course, which might be worked into the body of your paper through allusion or specific reference. In addition, it is usually wise to consult your teacher about a topic, as he can help you to limit it in a constructive manner or suggest a new slant. He may also mention a few key references, which will give you a good place from which to start your research.

CHAPTER 3

Research Sources

RESEARCH sources should be consulted as soon as you have chosen your topic: you should feel your way into a subject, not pounce on a topic simply because it is there. Acquaint yourself with your school library and with libraries in your community. And don't be bashful; no one knows everything. Librarians are on duty to answer *your* questions. Find out the location of reference room, card catalog, stacks, and reserve room; inquire about the card-catalog filing system and the shelving system. Once you feel reasonably comfortable in library country, you can begin to enjoy research.

Two kinds of source material are available to you: primary and secondary. You may want to use only primary sources, such as· an author's works. But if you have only a hazy idea of your subject, secondary sources—works of criticism—can be invaluable. Not only will they throw light on your subject, but they will present varying points of view, which you can support or contradict. (Don't be afraid to disagree: your reasoning power, if exercised, is every bit as good as another's.) Where do you find this secondary source material? First, try the card-catalog index under your author's name. Then try the following:

Encyclopedias

Special literary encyclopedias, such as *Cassell's Encyclopedia of Literature* and the *Oxford Clas-*

sical Dictionary, can serve as an introduction to your author and his tradition. You will find details of authors, titles, characters, themes, and terminology used in *The Reader's Companion to World Literature,* as well as in *The Oxford Companion* series to American, English, French, and classical literature.

Bibliographies

Bibliographies serve the same purpose as does the card-catalog subject index, only better; they often indicate the basic or best books on your subject. Each field has its own bibliography; you can find yours in a bibliography of bibliographies, such as the *Bibliographic Index.*

Periodical Indices

Periodical indices are catalogs of articles published in magazines. Indices that you may find useful include: *The Readers' Guide to Periodical Literature* (1900-) ; *Poole's Index to Periodical Literature* (1802-1906) ; and the *Publication of the Modern Language Association (PMLA Journal),* which has recent bibliographical as well as periodical information.

Footnotes

The footnotes in a comprehensive study of your author's works or his period may yield numerous leads to useful books.

And don't forget the dictionary. Keep one on

the table beside you while you read and *use* it.

Have you found mounds of material? Fine. But, before you get too far, verify the reliability of your sources by answering these questions:

(1) When was it written? Have there been important developments in your field since its copyright date?

(2) What are the author's qualifications? De Gaulle is not necessarily an authority on Molière.

(3) Does it approach your subject directly or from the side? Does it approach your subject?

(4) Is it biased? Does the author bear some personal grudge against your writer? Does his attitude show? Is his criticism of the work justifiable?

(5) Is it well footnoted? Critical works without footnotes are often perfectly honest and valid, but they may prove very difficult for you to use as reference sources.

There are many ways of gathering information other than through "pure research." If the author whom you are studying is still alive, write to him; ask him to comment on your topic or to clarify a point that is bothering you. Ask him if he has changed his mind and, if so, why. True, he may not answer, but isn't it worth a try? If he is dead, look for earlier editions of his work. How do they differ from your edition? Did the author make the changes? Why? Check your library's rare book room for some really early manuscripts—those of Shakespeare or Rabelais, for example. (Here, you are lucky if you are near a large library such as the Library of Congress or Harvard's Widener Library.) Even if you should find no significant textual changes, study the difference in manuscript reproduction between yesterday and today: paper, binding, marginal decoration. This may not help your research, but it could increase your general knowledge. Who knows? You may want to write a paper on early manuscripts some day. But, even if you don't see that in your future, think of the conversation you'll have to spark up your next date!

Perhaps there is an authority on your subject nearby, such as a college professor or a visiting lecturer. Ask him to spare a few minutes for you. Listen to his views; air your own. Do the same with your friends. No, they are not authorities; in fact, they probably know less about the subject than you do. But, in talking to them, you may be able to answer your own questions. Talking is itself a way of sifting facts, separating the wheat from the chaff. You want only wheat in your sack; the miller pays by the weight of the wheat, not the chaff.

For other leads, try to place your author in his historical setting. If you have access to a good library, you can usually find copies of books and newspapers published by your writer's contemporaries. (If he is still alive, the task will be all the easier.) Artists comment on their society and their times in their work, and factual accounts treating the same subjects as your literary material often provide illuminating counterpoint.

No, you don't *have* to do any of these things. But keep them in mind: they *could* be worth the effort. Remember, the term paper is not a punishment assignment (though it may seem so). It is an opportunity to widen your horizons, to make yourself at home in one constellation and to travel to others. Take advantage of your opportunity.

How much research should you do? That will depend on the type of paper that you have chosen. If you are brave, have confidence in your intellectual powers, and can rely upon your teacher or professor's tolerance, you may decide to use only the work or works that you are discussing. This, however, is a risky game. Since a teacher's primary purpose in assigning a paper is often to let you learn how to do research, some exploration of the field will be needed.

As a general rule, a paper ten pages long seems to require between five and ten sources; a fifteen-page paper, from twelve to sixteen sources; and a twenty-page paper, between eighteen and twenty-five. If you find that the number of books and periodicals that you are using varies significantly from these approximations, perhaps you had better stop to consider whether or not the information you have gathered will see you through a full paper.

Don't overwork yourself by taking down everything that passes before your eyes. Just because you took the trouble to look something up, that does not mean that it's necessarily worth anything to you. If it does bear on what you are going to say, don't take a chance on losing it, but *do* be selective. For longer passages, and maps or charts, you will often save time by making a photostatic copy, and some of the larger libraries provide machines for this purpose.

A final hint: avoid the temptation to examine that "one last book" if you think that you have already collected a representative cross section of material on your subject. At that point, your time will be better spent on the actual writing of the paper.

CHAPTER 4

Organization and Development

WHEN you have completed the search for the information that you will need to construct your paper, it is time to think about developing a system to gather together those facts and opinions which are pertinent to your hypothesis. The random pieces must be fitted together to form a logical and satisfying pattern.

The trick at this point is to make every moment of research time work for you. If you do a halfway job at the information-gathering stage, you may be forced to make a last-minute return trip to your sources to complete, supplement, or verify information that should have been noted the first time around. Sometimes you will find to your dismay that the material you need is now lost forever in the maze of the library shelves. Boring as it may seem at the time, thoroughness at this stage of the work can pay big dividends later on.

Bibliographical Notes

As you find books and articles that are relevant to your topic, make a 3″ x 5″ note-card for *each one,* listing author, title, publication data, call number, and page numbers of sections that you may wish to use. Do this as you go along, when the sources are right at hand; then, later on, the cards can be quickly shuffled into alphabetical or-

der to make the preparation of the bibliography
a snap.

Text and Commentary Notes

Taking notes as you read will make the eventual
organization of information less of a nerve-rack-
ing ordeal. Trap every glimmer of light you see on
a 3″ x 5″ card and note its source. Remember to
write down the page number and any other pertinent information, so that you will not have to
search for it later. Make sure that you have
enough material. The puzzle is tricky; you may
need every piece to solve it. If you already have
some picture of what you want to say, you will
find it useful to put headings on the cards, so that
you will know which ones go together.

If ideas occur to you while you are doing research, try to capture them on note-cards as well;
they may prove elusive tomorrow. Abbreviate
your notes as you wish, but keep this in mind:
abbreviations are as soon forgotten as invented.

Organization of Notes

When you are confident that you have sufficient
raw materials for your paper, you are ready to
start organizing the fruits of your labor into some
preliminary order.

Like any other task, a research paper requires
technique. Experience is the best teacher of methods to streamline the writing process; but "divide
and conquer" will aid you in organizing your information and arguments. Before trying to sys-

tematize, however, read through your notes several times to become thoroughly familiar with what you have discovered. Ignorance of the facts will prove a great handicap when you begin to make an outline or write the paper.

After reviewing your information, separate your notes into two or three categories, which correspond to the main areas of your paper. This division is a flexible one: you will probably change your mind several times before arriving at what seems to be the most logical arrangement. As you move the cards around, you will find that most information does seem to fall into a natural order; you will also be able to weed out any useless information. Organize each category by treating it as an entity, looking for introductory, developmental, and concluding sections. If your materials are weak in any of these areas, now is the time to do the extra research required. If everything seems in order, the categories can serve as the basis for your outline.

An efficient and logical organization of ideas, which builds toward a satisfying conclusion, is hard to achieve without a detailed outline. Structuring of information, while it may seem a nuisance if you are impatient to begin or are running out of time, will take much of the drudgery and frustration out of the writing process. The anxiety of scrambling through your notes in search of a fact that you *know* you had at some point can dismay even the most enthusiastic student. How much pleasanter it is to know what has to be said and to concentrate on the best way of presenting it. Furthermore, using an outline will keep you on the path of your argument, by eliminating the kind of interruptions and digressions that make so many term papers muddled and incompetent.

Much can also be said about the psychological benefits of making an outline. Having made the Herculean effort to organize many seemingly unrelated facts and opinions, you will have a certain confidence in the outcome of the paper. An outline gives you a timetable by which to measure the progress of your writing, for you can check off the various numerals and letters as you finish discussing them. In this way, you will know exactly how much of the work you have completed and how much you have left to write. A final point in praise of outlines: following an outline will enable you to write your paper in small chunks. This will make the whole task seem less formidable and will also lessen the risk of having to cope with an unmanageable amount of information later on.

The First Draft

The time for writing has come! If you have a clear idea of what you want to say, you are indeed in luck. If not, do not despair. Simply jot down all the conflicting ideas you have, then leave them while you have a leisurely Coke or a cup of coffee. When you come back, see what you can make out of the mess. You may be pleasantly surprised to find that there *is* order in your thoughts. Order or not, procrastination is not the answer. So gather your wits and your note-cards and force yourself to write a first draft.

Logic and clarity; clarity and logic: these are your guidelines. Repeat them till they penetrate your every brain cell—and your first draft. It may be bold and daring to set off on a journey knowing neither the goal nor the course to follow, but it *will not work* when writing a paper. There are less venturesome people on your trail here, and the object of the game is to let them catch you. Leave them clues as to your whereabouts in unified, coherent paragraphs; these they understand.

If your mind is functioning with particular efficiency at this time, get your ideas down and worry about editing them later. Don't lose a major idea by getting tangled in trying to set down your thoughts in flawless prose. That can come later. *Momentum* is the term-paper writer's greatest ally; if the thoughts are flowing, don't take a break to celebrate. It may take you hours to get back in the groove.

When your first draft is finished, then, and only then, should you rest. Put down your pen, get up, and do something entirely unrelated to term papers. Go anywhere; do anything. Let the distance between you and your paper widen till you are no longer a part of it. Then walk back to it and analyse it objectively. Find its faults and correct them. And remember: logic and clarity, clarity and logic. The most beautiful metaphor ever invented may not fit your paper; throw it out.

You may feel the need to walk away several times before you finish the final draft. Walk, then. But before you go, ask yourself: is it need, or only desire? If the latter, try to control it, to bend it to the matter at hand: completion.

The methodical work of recognizing the limits of your topic; knowing your facts; and adhering to a fairly formal plan for presenting information and argument is done to facilitate the actual writing process. All of the steps mentioned so far can be done in short stretches of time, at irregular intervals, thus minimizing the tedium that is involved in the preparation of a long paper and steering you to its completion without the usual panic. A paper that has been well planned in the manner already described should require only one draft, before typing, and can be composed at the rate of about two to four pages an hour. While writing it, constantly remind yourself: a paper must have a hypothesis. And concentrate on using your facts to state it, develop it, and prove its validity. The preliminary work you have done should free you to inject some flair into your writing and encourage an imaginative presentation, which will please both you and your teacher.

CHAPTER 5

Fundamentals of Form

HANDING your teacher a term paper that shows no sign of the discipline of form is not much better than giving him a bundle of note-cards. After all, he is probably quite familiar with your material: few students break any significant critical ground in these exercises. What he is looking for is proof that you have grasped the material well enough to present it in an organized and compelling fashion.

Used creatively, form imparts logic and dynamism to a paper, lends force to its arguments, and gives the reader a sense of satisfaction at its completion. Form is not necessarily a rigid pattern imposed upon your writing. It is an inherent quality of all good writing, for it points the reader in the direction you want him to go. Form is the structural manifestation of logic.

When you develop the form of your paper, let it be as creative as your thoughts. Bear in mind the kind of information you are trying to present and then decide how it can best be put in order. Some topics require a great deal of introductory material in order to acquaint the reader with the background that you consider necessary for a full understanding of the topic. Others may demand numerous examples to prove your thesis. The variations are endless, but all involve some sort of recognizable pattern, which serves as guide to both the author and the reader. The simplest cate-

gorical divisions include a STATEMENT OF PUR-
POSE, a DEVELOPMENT, and a CONCLUSION. The
statement of purpose may be modified to include a
brief introduction to the various themes that you
will be developing. The development may perhaps
include several subtopics, marked by formal or
implied chapter divisions, each of which has its
own purpose and conclusion in relation to the
over-all topic. The conclusion can be rendered
more effective by summarizing the arguments presented in the development to give your "conclusion" an air of inevitability. In any case, the form
you use should reflect the organization of your
outline, and succeed in giving your paper a feeling
of progression.

Making up footnotes and bibliography is probably the most tedious aspect of composing a term
paper. Like well-chosen accessories, however, they
can impart a look of polish and consequence to
your term paper. The most vexing problem you
will encounter when footnoting is determining
when you should or should not cite a reference.
Statistics, unusual or controversial dates (such as
that of Shakespeare's birth), and quotations
should always be footnoted. Opinions, critical
analysis by another, or interpretations should also
be cited. You can avoid using a formal footnote, if
you have already cited the work, by mentioning
the work of the author in the body of the text,
especially if the reference is well known or is one
that you have used frequently in the course. If you
are dealing with only one work, textual references
can be cited by merely including the page number
in parentheses after the statement.

To footnote or not to footnote: there will be
times when you are really stumped. It never hurts

to include them, of course, but a helpful rule to remember is: footnotes are usually unnecessary if the information is mentioned more than once in the text. Otherwise, be guided by the thought that footnotes are good insurance against suspicions of plagiarism.

Footnotes may be presented in several ways, depending on the requirements of your teacher. Some insist that the citations appear at the bottom of each page, whereas others may permit you to list them in a separate section at the end of your paper. The latter is infinitely easier for you, but harder for the reader. Several variations for presenting footnotes exist, but style is far less important than consistency. The author's full name, book title, place of publication, publisher, date of publication, and the page to which you are referring should appear in standard footnote form. The first line of the citation should be indented, and each footnote should be separated from the others by two spaces. Notes themselves should be single-spaced.

Mark Twain, *The Adventures of Huckleberry Finn* (New York: Washington Square Press, 1960), p. 57.

Notice in the example that the author's surname follows his Christian name (the opposite of the form for bibliographic citation). A comma divides the author's name from his work, and a period closes the footnote. Punctuation is not used between the title of the book and the parentheses containing the publication data. Other procedures include: underlining the book title, inserting a colon between the place of publication and the publisher's name, and putting a comma at the end of the parentheses. The form for periodicals resembles that for regular works, with a few exceptions. Usually the publisher and place of publication are not included, but the volume and issue numbers, separated by a comma, take their place after the titles. Most newspaper and magazine articles do not list an author, but, if they do, it should precede the title of the article and name of the publication. Examples of the most common types of form are shown as follows:

The Atlantic Monthly, Vol. X, 123 (1948), p. 65.

D. H. Lawrence, "Symbolism in Nature." *The Modern Poet,* Vol. III, 16 (Jan. 18, 1931), p. 23.

New York Times, July 12, 1911, p. 49.

For a work that is being cited more than once in your paper, there are two shortcuts that you may employ after you have formally listed the necessary information the first time it is used. The author's last name, followed by a comma and the page number is an easy method of reference, although if you are using more than one work by him, be sure to include a shorthand method of differentiating the various books. Example:

Hawthorne, p. 89.

or

Hawthorne, *Scarlet Letter,* p. 67.

If the footnote immediately preceding cites the same author and work as the one to which you are referring, the abbreviation *Ibid.* (always underlined) and the page number will be sufficient. Example:

Emerson, p. 78.
Ibid., p. 65.

The bibliography is an important clue to your teacher as to the amount of work and thought that have gone into the creation of your term paper. Most teachers are not easily fooled by the inclusion of numerous but irrelevant books, and many make a practice of checking for footnotes and references within the body of your paper in order to determine whether you actually have used the books listed. A long bibliography should be divided into the categories of SOURCES, SUPPLEMENTARY WORKS, and PERIODICALS AND NEWSPAPERS. The form for a bibliography entry differs from footnote form in only two ways; with the exception of the page number, each contains the same information. A bibliography entry lists the author's surname first; entries are arranged within categories in alphabetical order. Parentheses are omitted from around the publication data.

Dickens, Charles. *Bleak House.* New York: The New American Library of World Literature, Inc., 1964.

In the above example, note that the author's name and the title are followed by periods. The date and the publisher are separated by a comma.

CHAPTER 6

Putting Style in Your Paper

Literary style is a mysterious thing: no one can say why one writer's words leap from the page, while another's can scarcely limp. We can only give a few well-guessed hints.

Your writing style is the way in which *you* express your ideas. Whether you like it or not, the way in which you use language reveals your attitudes and capacities. Writing is, after all, a form of communication. Strive to make that communication as direct as possible. Armed with logic and clarity, good grammar, and your most objective eye, set out to prove your mettle on the field of communication.

In writing most papers, you will indeed be fighting a battle: whether to please yourself or please your professor. Rarely are both completely satisfied. But compromise is not necessarily weakness; it can even be victory if it results in a tone that is neither too subjective nor too objective, creative matter that does not run away with you. That you think clearly does not imply that you write clearly. Watch yourself carefully; a discerning eye is your best ally. Find out, if you can, the tone your professor prefers. If you can work with it comfortably, try it—this is one painless compromise. And it's not cheating. Most teachers, however, are pleased to find something in your paper that they have not prescribed, something you yourself have invented.

Take form, for instance. Simply because most

term papers are written in a prescribed form does not mean that yours must follow one. Try to present your paper in the form of a play: a paper on the psychological effect of truth in Ibsen's plays might lend itself to such a form. Characters from the plays might converse, explaining what truths they found, and how. Try to write as Ibsen would or, if that is too ambitious, write in your own words. If you fancy yourself a poet, and most of us do, try to write a paper in poetic form—iambic pentameter or blank verse. Model your criticism of Pope's "Rape of the Lock" on Pope's own poetic form. Try any medium you think you can handle. If you do it well, your professor is sure to be pleased. If you do it not so well, he will applaud your inventiveness. If you think it stinks, hand it in along with a paper in the prescribed form. Teachers are looking for the moment when your initiative will conquer their teachings and surge on to greater heights.

You should use initiative and inventiveness, but you should not attempt to invent your own language. As we have said before, it is wise to stay within the boundaries of clarity and good grammar. If your object is communication—and it should be—use the language your reader understands.

Here are a few rules to follow; perhaps they will help you to develop a style that is faithful to you.

(1) *Write what comes naturally.* Use the words and phrases that you hear in your mind, provided they make sense to your objective self. This does not give you license to use slang; slang has no place in term papers. The English language is rich; it will give you what you need.

(2) *Use enough nouns and verbs.* No matter

what adjectives or adverbs you use, they cannot revive a paper that lacks nouns and verbs.

(3) *Be concise.* Express your ideas in as few words as possible. You may be surprised at the power of concision.

(4) *Do not construct awkward phrases; avoid fancy words.* Do not dress up your speech. A face without make-up is far more attractive than an overpainted one.

(5) *Do not use stock phrases.* Use your mind; it has more to offer than all the stock phrases in the world. Remember inventiveness: it pays.

(6) *Write on your own level.* The plateau of writing should be at your intellectual level, neither below it nor above it. Write as though you had full command of your subject, not as though you were afraid of it or showing off your prowess.

(7) *Remember, you are writing for an audience of two.* You are one half of that audience, and you must please yourself. The professor is the other half; if you are honest with yourself and with him, he will respect you for it.

CHAPTER 7

Term Paper Tips

PERHAPS the greatest frustration that can result from a term paper is finding out, after you have gotten it back, that it has apparently been graded on the basis of the *lack* of some seemingly minor element, rather than of the presence of all your well-thought-out ideas. Since everyone puts a certain minimum degree of effort into his term paper, it is often the small finishing touches that separate the artists from the also-rans in the teacher's mind. Here are some of the ways to add polish to a paper:

(1) *Type it.* If it is at all feasible, type your paper. A teacher or professor cannot help but be impressed, favorably or unfavorably, by the visual impact of a paper. If it is neat, it is bound to look more logical and professional. For college students, typing is a definite must.

(2) *Make it look good.* Put a cover on a longer paper. Add a title page. If you have to cross out or insert a word on the final copy, consider retyping the page: corrections suggest mistakes.

(3) *Proofread it.* Why spend two weeks writing a paper and then not bother to go over it for grammatical, spelling, and typographical mistakes? Small errors here will annoy the reader and dull the impact of your ideas.

(4) *Be brave.* Impress your teacher by arguing against the consensus of opinion in your subject area. He is already familiar with what the critics

think, and he is bound to respect your intellectual initiative—if you have a valid point to make! Do not be presumptuous, however.

(5) *Mine the unworked veins.* Try discussing one of your author's lesser-known works. There will be less material to guide you, but you and your professor may find the result more interesting. Choosing such a subject will give you more of a chance to develop your own theories than will one about which a great deal of critical comment exists.

(6) *All that's gathered is not gold.* Just because you have got that quote or comment on a note-card does not mean that it has a place in your paper. If you are uncertain, discard it; it will probably detract from the conclusiveness of your argument.

(7) *Concise is nice.* Your ideas are like a boat; they will support only a certain number of words. If you overload them, they may sink into incoherence. Repetition may weaken your point and suggest that even you are not quite convinced. Teachers prefer the shorter paper that makes its points quickly and surely.

(8) *Take nothing for granted.* Never assume that your reader will be familiar with your subject. Although only your teacher will review your paper, it is supposed to be written for a hypothetical larger audience, whose expertise in the area of your topic cannot be taken for granted. Similarly, you must prove each step of your hypothesis; the teacher has no way of knowing why you left out a point. He may think you did not understand it.

(9) *A rich and titled paper.* Spend some time working on your title, either before or after the paper is completed. A good title may be amusing,

enigmatic, or erudite, but it should serve the dual purposes of defining your paper's scope to some degree and catching the reader's interest at the very beginning. The value of starting the reviewer off with a good impression of your intelligence and wit cannot be overstated.

(10) *Divide for dividends.* In papers over five or ten pages in length, some division of the text into chapters or segments can be very useful. This division not only highlights your ideas and aids the reader in his comprehension, but also forces you to make your points with greater care. You will be obliged to stop after making each point and look to see if you have stated it clearly and forcefully. If you have not proved your case at the end of a chapter, you cannot expect to catch it later on. Formal chapter breaks are not necessary; a line of asterisks is sufficient.

(11) *Cut your editing time.* If you are working through several drafts of your paper, you may find it expeditious to cut out the parts that need no further work and paste or tape them onto larger sheets of paper. You can then fill in the blanks between these segments on the larger sheets. Attaching note-cards directly to the draft will also conserve copying time.

PART II

TERM PAPER TOPICS

A Note on the Use of This Section

IN the pages that follow, you will find a selection of topics for term papers in the field of English. The examples range over the whole of the literary landscape: they are drawn from novels, poetry, and plays. Although the emphasis is on American and English works, you will also find a representative sampling from the Russian and other European writers as well as the Greek classics.

The topics, which were all devised by students, have been assembled both to inform you and to inspire you. They will give you a good indication of the many directions that a successful paper can take when a student uses his creative powers to instill life and imagination into it.

Each topic is intended only as a suggestion of what each paper might look like. In every one, the subject is viewed from a different literary angle. It is this variety of approach that you should take note of while you are reading through the topics. Examine all or most of them, not just the ones that deal with your assigned subject matter.

Actually, there are far more than a thousand topics on these pages, since the subject matter, the points of view, and the germinal ideas that constitute them can be recombined in an almost infinite variety of ways. If you see a good approach to one of Shakespeare's plays, why not try it on the play by Shaw or O'Neill that you have chosen or been assigned to write on? Can that study of Hemingway's characters be applied to one of Tennessee Williams' creations?

The goal of this book is not to provide you with a topic that will fulfill an academic requirement. Rather, its goal is to show you what can be done with any subject, once it is approached creatively. The vigor of creative life can be infused into every area of your paper, from the title to the closing paragraph. If you are being forced to pretend that you are a literary artist, why not go ahead and be one? If your interests seem miles away from the assignment, make them part of your paper. A good teacher admires honest thought more than any other quality in a student's work, so keep your grammar sound and your spelling respectable, but put something of yourself in your work. Both you and your teacher will enjoy it more.

Hopefully, as you go through the topics gathered here to guide you, you will find that some of them seem to suit your way of looking at things. Add to them, subtract, combine, emphasize, and create with their help a paper that says something in a way that you enjoy saying it.

Writing a good paper is never easy, but it doesn't have to be dull. Good luck.

The topics are divided into the major categories of ENGLISH LITERATURE, AMERICAN LITERATURE, EUROPEAN LITERATURE (including classical literature), and MISCELLANEOUS TOPICS. The English works are subdivided according to literary period;

the American, by century. All topics are in alphabetical order by author.

Topics marked (I) are considered to be the most simple, and those marked (III) the most sophisticated: however, these arbitrary ratings should not discourage you from using any topic that suits you.

The sample topic, below, illustrates the typographic arrangement used throughout. Note that the first paragraph, set in **bold face,** indicates the author and source. The next paragraph, set in SMALL CAPITAL LETTERS, gives you the suggested title of your paper. The paragraph outlining the scope of your paper is set in *italic.* And finally, in regular roman typeface, is the suggested approach you may follow.

SAMPLE TOPIC

**Author and
Source:**
**Christopher Marlowe:
*Doctor Faustus***

SUGGESTED
TITLE:
PRIDE IN *Doctor Faustus*

*Scope of
Your Paper:*
*Discuss the meaning and function
of pride in* Doctor Faustus.

Approach:
Discover the meaning of pride in
the characterizations and show
how prideful action charts the
course of the drama.   **(II)**

Term Paper Topics

ENGLISH LITERATURE

The Middle Ages (to 1485)

Geoffrey Chaucer: "The Nun's Priest's Tale"

THE USE OF SATIRE IN "THE NUN'S PRIEST'S TALE"

"The Nun's Priest's Tale" employs many types of satire on literary conventions, especially the conventions of the heroic narrative. Show how the satirical effects are achieved throughout the Tale.

Examine the language closely with the conventions of the classical epic in mind. Point out the contrasts achieved by Chaucer, especially those between style and subject matter. (II)

Geoffrey Chaucer: "The Pardoner's Tale"

CHAUCER'S COMMENT ON CHANGING SOCIAL STRUCTURES

Explore Chaucer's opinion of the social changes that he observed taking place around him.

Consider the poet's views on the growing strength of the Church and the gradual disintegration of the feudal system. In what ways does the poet reveal his opinions to the reader? (II)

The Elizabethan Period (1485–1603)

Thomas Hobbes: *The Leviathan*
THE HOBBESEAN VIEW OF MAN

What is Hobbes' essential point in The Leviathan?

How does Hobbes describe the nature of man? In the Hobbesean view, is man associated with the beasts or with the angels? How does this represent a marked change in theological thought? (I)

Christopher Marlowe: *Doctor Faustus*
THE RELIGIOUS IMPLICATIONS OF *Doctor Faustus*

Discuss the religious implications of the play.

How does the drama reveal a moral judgment of its characters? Discuss in terms of metaphor, characterization, and dramatic structure.   (II)

Christopher Marlowe: *Doctor Faustus*
MARLOWE: AN ATHEIST?

During his lifetime, Marlowe was thought by many to be an atheist. Consider evidence within Doctor Faustus *to support or refute this theory.*

What is Faustus' professed attitude toward God? What is his attitude toward the Devil? With the climax of the play in mind, how do you think Marlowe regarded his character, Faustus?   (I)

Christopher Marlowe: *Doctor Faustus;* Thomas Mann: *Doctor Faustus*
DOCTOR FAUSTUS IN MANN AND MARLOWE

A comparison of Marlowe's play Doctor Faustus *with Mann's novel of the same name.*

Both works are based on the same (German)
legend: Marlowe's, overtly; Mann's, thematically.
In what ways does the story of Leverkuhn resemble that of Faustus? What themes do they hold in
common? How do the works differ in scope?
Where Mann's work touches on wider themes,
does the Faustus story still have any relevance?
(III)

Thomas Nashe: *The Unfortunate Traveller*

THE PICARESQUE HERO IN NASHE'S *The Unfortu-
nate Traveller*

*Attempt to define "picaresque hero," using Thomas
Nashe's hero as an example.*

Consider the unity of the work. Is there any plot?
What single factor makes the work function as a
whole? Is the reader's interest sustained by
subtlety of characterization or by diversity of
action?   (I)

Plutarch: *Parallel Lives;*
William Shakespeare: *Antony and Cleopatra;*
T. S. Eliot: *The Waste Land*

THE DESCRIPTION OF CLEOPATRA IN PLUTARCH,
SHAKESPEARE, AND T. S. ELIOT

*Compare Plutarch's account of Cleopatra with
Enobarbus' in* Antony and Cleopatra *(Act II,
scene ii). Compare Shakespeare's version with
that of T. S. Eliot in* The Waste Land *("A Game
of Chess").*

Show how Shakespeare greatly enlarges the characterization of Cleopatra by subtle changes in

North's translation of Plutarch's text. Show how Eliot uses Shakespeare's basic text for a completely different purpose.   **(II)**

William Shakespeare: *Antony and Cleopatra*
THE TRAGEDY OF ENOBARBUS

The dilemma and subsequent death of Enobarbus parallels the decline and fall of Antony. What is the importance of the Enobarbus episode?

Antony is caught between the epicurean life of Egypt and the military rigors of Rome. In what way is Enobarbus' position similar to Antony's? Each character makes a choice. How do they differ in that choice?   **(II)**

William Shakespeare: *Antony and Cleopatra*
ANTONY'S GENIUS FOR FRIENDSHIP

"Antony is the most likable of Shakespeare's tragic characters." Do you agree? What evidence is there within the play of Antony's genius for friendship?

Consider the significance of Enobarbus' desertion. Why is Eros introduced? Compare Antony with Octavius Caesar. Do the differences in their personalities reflect the differences between Rome and Egypt?   **(II)**

William Shakespeare: *Hamlet*
HAMLET'S INABILITY TO ACT

Throughout the play, Hamlet is characterized by the inability to take decisive action. Discuss.

Does Hamlet believe in the tale of his father's ghost? If so, what are the reasons for such tests as having the play enacted before his uncle? Why does he leave Denmark, and what are the circumstances of his return? What event causes him at last to avenge his father?   (I)

William Shakespeare: *Hamlet*
THE ART OF THE DRAMA IN *Hamlet*

Through the medium of the theater, the reader is allowed to become more familiar with the character of Hamlet than he could with that of someone in real life. Discuss.

Consider such techniques as soliloquy, the telescoping of time, and the reader's "bird's-eye view" of the action.   (I)

William Shakespeare: *Hamlet, Macbeth*
THE USE OF THE SUPERNATURAL IN *Hamlet* AND *Macbeth*

Compare the role of Hamlet's father's ghost in Hamlet *with the role of the witches in* Macbeth.

Contrast the influences of these supernatural events upon the characters in each case. Do these events determine the actions of any of the characters in either case?   (I)

William Shakespeare: *Hamlet*
Hamlet: ESPIONAGE AS HIGH CAMP

An analysis of the motivating forces in the play.

The object of this paper is to demonstrate the plausibility of the theory that both Hamlet and

Claudius have political ideas of prime motive proportions. The cause of Hamlet's tragedy should be shown to lie in the necessity and the impossibility of reconciling his private and public selves. (III)

William Shakespeare: *Henry IV, Part I*

THE REDEMPTION OF PRINCE HAL

Consider any changes in Prince Hal's attitude toward his friends at the Boar's Head and toward his princely responsibilities during the course of Henry IV, Part I.

Explore the nature of his friendship with Falstaff and his attitude toward Hotspur. Consider the importance of the tapsters who call the Prince the "King of Courtesy." (I)

William Shakespeare: *Henry IV, Part I*

FALSTAFF'S MORALITY

Falstaff is a liar, a thief, a lecher, a glutton, and a coward, and yet he is one of Shakespeare's most popular characters. What constitutes his appeal? Confine your discussion to the portrait of Falstaff in Henry IV, Part I.

Consider Falstaff's own explanations for his conduct. What, for example, does Prince Hal see in him? (II)

William Shakespeare: *Henry IV, Part II*

THE REPUDIATION OF FALSTAFF

In Henry IV, Part II, *Prince Hal, now King Henry, repudiates Falstaff, a character with whom the reader has come to sympathize. Is this repudiation justifiable?*

Does Shakespeare prepare the reader for Hal's denial of Falstaff? How does Shakespeare's presentation of Falstaff in *Part II* differ from that in *Part I?*   (II)

William Shakespeare: *Julius Caesar, Coriolanus, Antony and Cleopatra*

STATECRAFT IN SHAKESPEARE'S ROMAN PLAYS

Each of the Roman plays is a sort of lesson in statecraft. In what respects is this true?

Consider the relation of the individual to the state in each of these plays. How does the conflict shift from play to play? What is the role played by the commoner in each case?   (III)

William Shakespeare: *Julius Caesar*

SUPERNATURAL EVENTS IN *Julius Caesar*

In what way do supernatural events foreshadow later happenings in Julius Caesar? *Do these events give you a deeper insight into the characters?*

Consider the storm, the lion in the forum, the soothsayer, and the ghost in *Julius Caesar*.   (I)

William Shakespeare: *King Lear*

THE FOOL IN *King Lear*

What dramatic purpose does the Fool serve?

Is the Fool a fool indeed? What is the Fool's relation to Lear? What attitude toward the dramatic situation does the Fool represent throughout?

Why does Shakespeare give such an important role to a "fool"? (II)

William Shakespeare: *King Lear*
LEAR AND GLOUCESTER

The story of Lear and his daughters is paralleled throughout by the story of Gloucester and his sons. Unravel the intricacies of this parallelism. How do the two plots interrelate?

Compare the tragic mistake of Gloucester and that of Lear. How does Gloucester's physical blindness compare with Lear's spiritual blindness? What realization do Gloucester and Lear share at the end of the play? (I)

William Shakespeare: *King Lear*
JUSTICE IN *King Lear*

At one point, Lear protests that he is "more sinned against than sinning." What consolation does Shakespeare provide to mollify for Lear the apparent injustices of this world?

Compare the various attitudes toward fate evinced by Edmund, Gloucester, Albany, and Lear. (II)

William Shakespeare: *King Lear*
"HOW SHARPER THAN A SERPENT'S TOOTH"

What is King Lear's great realization during the course of the play?

Consider the storm scene. What basic attitude toward life does Lear seem to profess in that

scene? How does this attitude differ from that in
Act I, scene 1? How does it relate to the climax of
the play?   (II)

William Shakespeare: *Macbeth*

THE WITCHES IN *Macbeth*

What role do the witches actually play in Macbeth? Do they in fact influence Macbeth's actions?

How does Macbeth react to his first encounter
with the witches? Consider Lady Macbeth's reaction to her husband's letter. What attention does
Macbeth give to their subsequent prophecies? (I)

William Shakespeare: *Macbeth*

THE CONSCIENCE OF MACBETH AND LADY MACBETH

*Show that, as the play progresses, Macbeth heeds
the dictates of his conscience less and less, while
the conscience of Lady Macbeth creates in her an
ever-increasing despair, which leads to her eventual death.*

What is Lady Macbeth's evaluation of her husband before the murders? after the murders?
What is the significance of her "Nought's had,
all's spent" or her "Out, damned spot" soliloquy?
                                                      (I)

William Shakespeare: *Measure for Measure, Othello*

OTHELLO AND LEONTES: A STUDY OF JEALOUSY

*In simplest terms, Leontes and Othello are both
motivated by jealousy. Is there any difference between their respective passions?*

Each character suspects his wife of infidelity. Compare the grounds for suspicion in each case. In what way does the jealousy of Leontes affect characters other than Polixenes and Hermione? Does Othello act in a similar fashion? Is Othello motivated by jealousy or by a misdirected sense of responsibility? (II)

William Shakespeare: *Othello*

THE LOVE OF DESDEMONA

Try to correlate Othello's actions with the sort of love that he shares with Desdemona.

Consider carefully Othello's own account of his courtship of Desdemona in Act I. In that account, what particular quality in him does Desdemona seem especially to admire? In respect to that quality, is Othello consistent throughout the play? (I)

William Shakespeare: *Othello, King Lear*

IAGO'S MOTIVES

Iago is a villain of satanic proportions. What, if any, are his motivations?

What explanation does Iago himself give? Compare him with Edmund in *King Lear*. Does a study of Iago's character cast light upon Othello? Which is the stronger character? (III)

William Shakespeare: *Othello*

THE CITY AND THE ISLAND

What necessitates a change of scene from Venice to Cyprus? Why are the scenes in Venice included in the play?

With what social values is Venice associated in Othello's mind? Who is in charge of the city? Does the change of scene to Cyprus correspond to a change in social structure? What is the dramatic effect of this change?   (II)

William Shakespeare: *Richard II*

Richard II: PORTRAIT OF A POET

Shakespeare's portrayal of Richard II is in many respects a portrait of a poet or playwright.

Consider Richard's manner of arbitrating the dispute between Bolingbroke and Mowbray. Why does Richard stop the tournament? In the abdication scene, why does he call for the mirror? Notice his tendency to make puns and manipulate words. Review Richard's final soliloquy.   (III)

William Shakespeare: *Richard II*

THE MORAL IMPLICATIONS OF USURPATION IN *Richard II*

Shakespeare suggests that Bolingbroke's usurpation has moral as well as political implications. What are these implications?

Consider the "sun" symbolism that surrounds Richard. Are there Christian symbols as well? Keep in mind the doctrine of the divine right of kings. Consider the prophecies spoken by Carlisle and Richard in the fourth act.   (II)

William Shakespeare: *Romeo and Juliet*

Romeo and Juliet: A STUDY IN LOVE

Compare Romeo's love for Rosalinde, as he de-

scribes it in the first act, with his later love for Juliet.

Make a close study of the language Romeo uses to describe his love for Rosalinde. Compare it with the language of Shakespeare's love sonnets. How does the former speech differ from his famous speech to Juliet? Consider Juliet's speech concerning the nature of a lover's vow. (II)

William Shakespeare: *Romeo and Juliet*

Romeo and Juliet IN OUR TIME

Underlying Shakespeare's drama is a lesson that is universally applicable, even to our own time. Construct a twentieth-century setting for Shakespeare's plot.

Consider race relations, politics, or the international scene as possible elements in a setting. (I)

William Shakespeare: *The Tempest*

CONCEPTS OF THE COMMONWEALTH IN *The Tempest*

Compare and contrast the various views of the commonwealth found in The Tempest.

Contrast Gonzalo's dream of the ideal commonwealth with the machinations of Sebastian and Antonio and those of Stephano and Trinculo. How does Prospero govern his island? (II)

William Shakespeare: *The Tempest*

TRANSFORMATION IN *The Tempest*

How is evil transmitted into good in the course of the play?

What changes come about in each character, and especially in Prospero? What are the sources of these changes? Why does Prospero wish to return? (I)

William Shakespeare: *The Tempest*

THE USE OF SONG IN *The Tempest*

Explore the dramatic significance of song in The Tempest. *What function does it have?*

Which of the characters sing the songs? How do the songs of one character differ from those of another? Do these differences mirror basic personality differences? Do the songs reflect the dramatic situation? (III)

William Shakespeare: *The Tempest, Measure for Measure, A Winter's Tale*

THE MELLOWING OF SHAKESPEARE IN THE LATER ROMANCES

The Tempest, Measure for Measure, *and* A Winter's Tale *seem to reflect a new gentleness of attitude toward human beings on the part of the playwright. Within the plays, what evidence points to this mellowing?*

Consider the compassionate sense of justice found in *Measure for Measure* and the portrait of mankind drawn in *The Tempest*. (I)

William Shakespeare: *The Tempest*

A SHAKESPEAREAN SELF-PORTRAIT

What evidence in The Tempest *might lead you to believe that the character Prospero is, in fact, a portrait of Shakespeare himself?*

Consider the fashion in which Prospero calls forth spirits to "enact" his "fancy." Review the scene in which he renounces his magical powers.   (II)

William Shakespeare: *Troilus and Cressida*

Troilus and Cressida: A SHAKESPEAREAN SATIRE

In writing this play, Shakespeare seemed bitter and almost cynical. Unravel the satiric implications and suggest a possible explanation for them.

Consider the portrayal of Troilus's love for Cressida. Do Achilles and Ajax seem like heroic figures? Who, in fact, is the hero of this play? Who is the main character?   (II)

William Shakespeare: *The Two Gentlemen of Verona*

LOVE COMEDY IN *The Two Gentlemen of Verona*

Proteus' faithlessness toward his love, Julia, and his betrayal of his friend Valentine might easily be a subject for tragedy. In this case, it is a subject for comedy. Why?

Consider the sort of love that Shakespeare is describing in this comedy. Carefully review Proteus' courtship of Silvia. Does this study suggest the meaning of "courtly love"? Compare Proteus' love for Silvia with Romeo's love for Rosalinde.   (I)

William Shakespeare: "Venus and Adonis"

SATIRE IN "VENUS AND ADONIS"

In what respect is "Venus and Adonis" a satiric poem? What particular values is the poet satirizing?

Study the description of Venus. Which of her characteristics has Shakespeare exaggerated? Consider Adonis in the same way. Compare the dramatic situation of Shakespeare's poem with the situation in a love sonnet by a different poet (Drayton would be a good choice). How is the situation reversed?   (I)

William Sheridan: *The Rivals, School for Scandal*

SHERIDAN'S USE OF NAMES

An examination of the use of names in Sheridan.

Consider the names that Sheridan uses. How do they fit the characters? What is their dramatic function?   (I)

Sir Phillip Sidney: *The Defense of Poesy*

SIDNEY: THE HIERARCHY OF LEARNING

Explore the distinctions that Sidney makes between historian, philosopher, and poet.

What common goal do the philosopher, the historian, and the poet share? In what way does each pursue this goal? In Sidney's view, which of the three studies is the most effective and rewarding? Why?   (I)

Sir Phillip Sidney: *The Defense of Poesy*

THE MORAL POSITION OF THE POET IN SIDNEY'S *The Defense of Poesy*

In his Defense, *Sidney suggests that the function of poetry is not only aesthetic but also moral. In what respect is this true?*

Consider Sidney's account of the Fall of Man. What were the consequences of that Fall? What is the significance of "speech" and "reason"? In what sense is the poet a "maker"? (II)

Edmund Spenser: "The Garden of Adonis," "The Cantos of Mutability"

THEME AND STRUCTURE IN "THE GARDEN OF ADONIS" AND "THE CANTOS OF MUTABILITY"

Compare and contrast the theme, metaphors, and texture of the poems.

Relate theme to metaphor and the use of language. (II)

Edmund Spenser: *The Faerie Queene*

LEWD AND HEALTHY LOVE IN *The Faerie Queene*

Discuss the representations of lewd and healthy love, in terms of metaphor and action, in Books II, III, and IV of The Faerie Queene.

How does Spenser indicate in the course of narrative, through incident and metaphor, his judgment of these forms of love? (II)

Edmund Spenser: *The Faerie Queene;* John Milton: *Paradise Lost*

THE SIN OF SENSUAL PLEASURE

Consider the description of the Bower of Bliss in the second book of The Faerie Queene. *What particular aspect of that description suggests the immorality that the poet is trying to point out? Why does Sir Guyon destroy the Bower?*

Compare the description of the Bower with Milton's description of Eden in the fourth book of *Paradise Lost.*   (II)

Edmund Spenser: *The Faerie Queene*

THE ALLEGORY OF *The Faerie Queene,* BOOK VI

Show how the incidents of Book VI exhibit the traits of courtesy. What is the meaning of the pastoral interlude in the middle of the course of the story?

Keep the ideal of courtesy in mind as you try to understand the human knight on his quest.   (III)

Edmund Spenser: "The Shepherd's Calendar," "Mother Hubbard's Tale"

SATIRE AND IDEALISM IN "THE SHEPHERD'S CALENDAR" AND "MOTHER HUBBARD'S TALE"

Compare and contrast the uses of idealism and satire in these works.

What is the precise relationship, thematically and structurally, of idealism to satire in each work? How do the uses of satire and idealism determine a different character in each poem?   (II)

Edmund Spenser: "The Shepherd's Calendar" Sir Phillip Sidney: *The Defense of Poesy*

AN EXPLICATION OF THE OCTOBER ECLOGUE OF "THE SHEPHERD'S CALENDAR"

Comment upon the discussion of the goal and rewards of poetry found in the eclogue.

Consider the significance of Spenser's own poetic career. Why did he begin by writing pastorals and end by writing an epic? In this eclogue, is there anything to suggest Spenser's plan to write *The Faerie Queene?* Consult Sidney's *The Defense of Poesy* as to the hierarchy of poetic forms. (II)

The Seventeenth Century (1603–1660)

John Donne: "The Sunne Rising"

DONNE'S POETIC TECHNIQUE IN "THE SUNNE RISING"

How does the poet present experience? How are the conceits of the poem related to one another? What is the force of the poet's voice guiding the poem?

Examine each stanza to see how they are related to one another in terms of image and theme. What is the meaning of the whole? (III)

John Donne: "The Flea"

PROLIFERATION OF AN IMAGE

A discussion of how the central image is developed in Donne's poem "The Flea."

Show how the speaker in the poem draws more and more implications from the image of the flea during the course of the narrative. How does he bring in ethical, moral, religious, and amatory considerations? How does the flea figure in the dramatic situation of the poem? (II)

John Donne, Robert Herrick, Andrew Marvell: poetry

POETIC ATTITUDES: DONNE, HERRICK, AND MARVELL

Show how the differing treatments of the themes of time and mutability and the lover's persuasion, by these three poets, reveal their various attitudes toward life and their conceptions of the function of poetry.

Examine one or two representative lyrics by the three authors, explicate them, and contrast the points made by the three. In each case, what does the poem imply about the poet's conception of the proper function of poetry? (I)

John Donne, Ben Jonson: poetry

THE POETIC STYLES OF JOHN DONNE AND BEN JONSON

Contrast the two poetic styles that arose at the beginning of the seventeenth century, using John Donne and Ben Jonson as examples of the two opposing styles.

Compare Donne's choice of imagery with that of Jonson. How does the subject matter of the two differ? Consider the role of the poet as narrator in each case. (II)

John Donne: "The Sunne Rising"; Christopher Marlowe: "The Passionate Shepherd to His Love"

THE LOVE POETRY OF DONNE AND MARLOWE

Using "The Passionate Shepherd to His Love," by Christopher Marlowe, as an example of conventional Elizabethan love poetry, and John Donne's "The Sunne Rising" as a type of the metaphysical love poem, contrast the Elizabethan and metaphysical styles.

Consider the use of imagery in each example. How does Marlowe's choice of metaphor differ from Donne's?   (II)

John Donne: *Holy Sonnets*

JOHN DONNE AND RELIGIOUS EXPERIENCE

In his religious poetry, how does Donne view the relation between God and man? In what way does he approach God and religious experience in general?

Consider Donne's *Holy Sonnets*. What sort of language is used there to describe God? and man?
                                                                 (II)

John Donne: *Songs* and *Sonnets*

WHAT IS A METAPHYSICAL CONCEIT?

What peculiarities distinguish the metaphysical conceit from other poetic metaphors?

Confine your study to the poetry of John Donne. Consider his unique use of imagery—such as comparing love to a geographer's compass. Does this sort of imagery explicate the subject of a poem or does it reflect the personality of the poet?   (I)

George Herbert: *The Temple*

THE EMBLEMATIC VERSE OF GEORGE HERBERT

In what sense of the word is Herbert's poetry emblematic?

How do the rhyme scheme, diction, and meter of a Herbert poem stand for the actual message of

the poem? In "Denial," the mental distraction of
the narrator is emphasized by irregularity of the
rhymes. Consider "The Altar" and "Easter
Wings."   (III)

Robert Herrick, Ben Jonson: poetry

HERRICK AND JONSON: A COMPARISON

*Compare the poetry of Robert Herrick with that
of Ben Jonson.*

Notice similarities of style with respect to rhyth-
mic and metric correctness. How does the subject
matter differ? What basic stylistic similarity do
these two poets share which distinguishes them
from the school of John Donne.   (II)

Robert Herrick: "To the Virgins, to Make Much of Time"; Andrew Marvell: "To a Coy Mistress"

THE COY MISTRESS IN MARVELL AND HERRICK

*Compare Marvell's "To A Coy Mistress" with
Herrick's "To the Virgins, to Make Much of
Time."*

Discuss the radical differences of style and approach between these poems. Do these differences
suggest the separation between the school of John
Donne and the school of Ben Jonson?   (II)

Thomas Hobbes: *The Leviathan;* John Milton: *Paradise Lost*

THE NATURE OF MAN: HOBBES AND MILTON

*Compare the Hobbesean view of human nature,
expressed in* The Leviathan, *with the Miltonic
view, in* Paradise Lost.

Consider Milton's account of the Creation, in Book VII of *Paradise Lost*. Why did God create man? What is man's position in relation to the angels and the beasts? How does this contrast with the Hobbesean view? (II)

Ben Jonson: poetry

JONSONIAN INNOVATION

Discuss the stylistic innovations in the poetry of Ben Jonson.

Compare a love poem by Ben Jonson with a love poem by an earlier Elizabethan (Christopher Marlowe's "The Passionate Shepherd to His Love" would be a good choice), and with a love poem by John Donne. How do the imagery, diction, and stance of the narrator differ in each case? (II)

Ben Jonson: *Every Man in His Humour, Every Man Out of His Humour*

THE JONSONIAN THEORY OF HUMOURS

What is the theory of humours?

Consider Jonson's comic technique in the "humour" plays. How does this technique break with tradition? How is it achieved? (III)

Andrew Marvell: "Upon Appleton House"

INTRUSIONS INTO SOLITUDE IN "UPON APPLETON HOUSE"

What are the destructive forces in this poem, and how are they annulled by the poet?

Define the meaning of each destructive element.

What is the ultimate source of peace for the poet?
(II)

Andrew Marvell: "The Garden"

POWER IN MARVELL'S "THE GARDEN"

*What are the attractions of the garden? How does
sensuous language express its power over the
mind of the poet, which becomes translated into a
physical detainment?*

Examine each stanza closely, looking for the
sources of the poet's attraction to the garden.
Evaluate the power of the rich language itself in
terms of the poem's meaning.   (III)

John Milton: *Comus*

PLATONISM IN *Comus*

*Point to evidences of Platonic philosophy in
Comus.*

Consider the elder brother's speech (line 455 on).
What is meant by "soul's essence"? How is this
state achieved? What role does sensuality play?
How do these ideas relate to the philosophy of
Plato?   (III)

John Milton: *L'Allegro, Il Penseroso*

METRICAL MANIPULATION IN *L'Allegro* AND *Il
     Penseroso*

*Read these two poems aloud and you will notice
that* L'Allegro *reads much more quickly than* Il
Penseroso. *In terms of metrics, how is this
achieved?*

Consider such metrical devices as polysyllabic diction, alliteration, caesura, and the use of open vowel sounds. (II)

John Milton: *L'Allegro, Il Penseroso*

L'Allegro AND *Il Penseroso:* A STUDY IN MOOD

Consider the interrelation of these two poems. What are they really about?

These poems trace a day in the life of a happy extrovert and then of a contemplative introvert. Do the poems celebrate personality or mood? (II)

John Milton: "Lycidas," "On the Death of Damon"

"LYCIDAS" AND "ON THE DEATH OF DAMON" COMPARED

These two poems are of the same poetic genre. They are quite different, however. Explore this difference.

Who is Damon? Who is Lycidas? What is the relationship between the poet and his subject in each case? Does this difference explain a difference in the total effect of the poems? (III)

John Milton: *Of Education*

MILTON'S ACADEMY

Consider the school proposed by Milton in Of Education. *Would you endorse his proposal?*

Do you approve of the heavy emphasis Milton places on humanitarian studies and of the deemphasizing of science? Do you think it is possible for a student to progress at the rate that Milton suggests? Do you believe in the basic philosophy underlying his academy? (I)

John Milton: *Paradise Lost*

MILTONIC ANGELS

Throughout Paradise Lost, *Milton takes pains to define the physiology of angels. In Milton's opinion, what is an angel like?*

Of what substance are angels made? Can they change shape? How do angels nourish themselves? Are they male or female? (I)

John Milton: *Paradise Lost*

SATAN'S TRANSFORMATION

Discuss Satan's diminution in stature in Paradise Lost.

In Book I, Satan is pictured as a "sultan" or "emperor." In Book IV, he is "squat like a toad." Discuss the significance of this diminution in stature. Does Satan seem more grand in the setting of Hell than on earth? Does Milton suggest a gradual transformation from archangel to archfiend? (II)

John Milton: *Paradise Lost*

MILTON'S POETIC STYLE

Pick a passage from Paradise Lost *and try to characterize its manner and style. How does the mode of expression relate to the "grand theme" of the poem?*

Examine allusion, diction, and syntax. How does the structure of the verse relate to the moral meaning of the work?   (I)

John Milton: *Paradise Lost*

PRIDE IN *Paradise Lost*

Discuss the meaning and function of pride in the poem.

Define "pride" in this context and show how prideful action affects the course of the epic. Find examples of the depiction of pride and the judgment of it in metaphor and language as well as in characterization.   (II)

John Milton: *Paradise Lost, Paradise Regained*

THE GROWTH OF SATAN

In what ways does Satan change during the course of Paradise Lost *and* Paradise Regained?

Consider any physical changes in Satan that seem to take place in *Paradise Lost.* Consider also Satan's capacity for deception. In what way does that capacity increase during the course of these two poems?   (II)

John Milton: *Paradise Lost, Paradise Regained*

SATAN'S TEMPTATIONS OF CHRIST AND OF EVE COMPARED

Compare Satan's temptations of Christ in Paradise Regained *with his temptations of Eve in* Paradise Lost.

What does Satan offer in each case? In what respect are both temptations a test of obedience to God?   (II)

John Milton: *Paradise Lost*

DRAMATIC ELEMENTS IN *Paradise Lost*

What dramatic elements can you find in the structure of Paradise Lost?

Why does the poem begin with Satan on the burning lake? Why is the story of Satan's rebellion told in flashback? What is significant in the juxtaposition of Satan's rebellion (Book VI) with God's Creation of the world (Book VII)?   (II)

John Milton: *Paradise Lost, Doctrine and Discipline of Divorce*

MILTON'S ATTITUDE TOWARD WOMEN

Samuel Johnson observed that Milton seemed scornful of women. What evidence can you find of this attitude in Milton's works?

Consider Milton's description of the relationship between Adam and Eve. For further evidence, consult Milton's *Doctrine and Discipline of Divorce*. In Milton's terms, what is the role of woman in her relation to man?   (II)

John Milton: *Paradise Lost*

MILTON'S UNIVERSE

Describe Milton's picture of the universe, as presented in Paradise Lost.

What is the earth's relation to Heaven and Hell? How is the earth suspended? What fills the space between Heaven, earth, and Hell?   (I)

John Milton: *Paradise Lost*
MESSIAH IN *Paradise Lost*

Who is Messiah, and how did he gain his preeminence?

When and by whom was Messiah created? What is his relation to God? What is his relation to man? What is the significance of the word "merit," which is often associated with this figure? How does "merit" account for Messiah's position in the chain of being?   (II)

John Milton: *Paradise Lost, Christian Doctrine*
THE DOCTRINE OF CHRISTIAN LIBERTY

According to Milton in Paradise Lost, *how is the state of perfect freedom achieved?*

In what way are Adam and Eve more free before their fall than after? Answer the same question about Satan. What is to be achieved through strict obedience to God?   (III)

John Milton: *Paradise Lost;* Virgil: *Aeneid*
ADAM AND AENEAS AS HEROES

Compare and contrast these two characters as heroes.

What makes each a hero? How does the concept of heroism in each work relate to larger themes?   (II)

John Milton: *Paradise Regained*

THE CONFUSION OF SATAN IN *Paradise Regained*

In what way does Satan misunderstand Christ's intentions on earth?

Prophets had said that a man would come to rule the world and that his kingdom would be without end. How does Satan interpret the word "kingdom"? What, in fact, is Christ's intention? How does this confusion explain Satan's attempts and failures to tempt Christ?   (II)

John Milton: *Samson Agonistes*

REGENERATION IN *Samson Agonistes*

Explore the spiritual transformation that Samson undergoes in Milton's dramatic poem.

Contrast Samson's attitude toward God at the beginning of the play with his attitude at the end. In the same way, consider Samson's attitude toward his own mission in life. What is the significance of his repudiation of Dalilia?   (II)

John Milton: *Samson Agonistes*

GREEK TRAGEDY IN ENGLISH

In what way does Milton's Samson Agonistes resemble a Greek tragedy?

Consider Milton's dramatic technique. Are the unities observed? Is there any suspense, or does the reader already know the outcome of the plot? How did Milton achieve such a close approximation of Greek tragedy within a totally Christian play?   (II)

John Milton, William Shakespeare: sonnets

THE SONNETS OF MILTON AND SHAKESPEARE COMPARED

Compare Milton's use of the sonnet form with Shakespeare's.

In terms of rhyme scheme, how do the sonnets of these two poets differ? What effect does this change of form have upon the presentation of the subject matter? Some have said that a Miltonic sonnet reads like a paragraph of blank verse. How is this effect achieved? (II)

Thomas Otway: *Venice Preserved*

THE ESSENTIAL CONFLICT IN *Venice Preserved*

The "passion versus reason" conflict was a standard theme for the seventeenth-century playwrights. Show how Otway adapted this essential conflict for Venice Preserved.

What are Jaffier's opposing allegiances? (II)

The Restoration (1660–1798)

Joseph Addison and Sir Richard Steele: *The Spectator*

MORALITY IN *The Spectator*

Both Addison and Steele were conscious moralists. What moral point of view did they foster?

What is the role of moderation, reason, and good taste? (I)

James Boswell: *The Life of Johnson;*
Samuel Johnson: any prose work

POVERTY IN THE LIFE OF SAMUEL JOHNSON

What do you think was the influence of poverty on the critical, moral, and social attitudes of Dr. Johnson?

As a start, consider Johnson's repudiation of the patron system.   (II)

Lord Chesterfield: *Letters to His Son;*
James Boswell: *Life of Johnson*

THE SOCIAL MAN: SAMUEL JOHNSON AND LORD CHESTERFIELD

Compare the views of Johnson and Lord Chesterfield on the social man.

Consider the relative importance accorded by each to intelligence, wit, and good manners.   (I)

John Bunyan: *Pilgrim's Progress*

BUNYAN'S USE OF LANDSCAPE

Discuss the use of landscape in Pilgrim's Progress.

Analyze Bunyan's use of landscape in his allegory. Does this make sense to you? Why?   (I)

Edmund Burke: *Reflection on the Revolution in France*

EDMUND BURKE: THE CONSERVATIVE VIEW

What is Burke's attitude toward cultural heritage?

In Burke's view, what is the danger of political revolution?   (II)

Fanny Burney: *Evelina*

THE SATIRIC STANCE IN *Evelina*

In what way is the dramatic situation of Evelina *suited to satire?*

Is Evelina a sort of "innocent abroad"? In what respects is this true?   (II)

William Congreve: *The Way of the World, Love for Love*

WIT IN CONGREVE

An investigation of Congreve's use of wit.

What is wit? How does Congreve use it?   (I)

George Crabbe: "The Village"; Oliver Goldsmith: "Deserted Village"

CRABBE AND GOLDSMITH: TWO VIEWS OF THE RURAL LIFE

Compare Crabbe's "The Village" with Goldsmith's "Deserted Village."

Consider the contrasting attitudes toward rural life that these two poems reflect.   (II)

Daniel Defoe: *Robinson Crusoe*

REALISM IN *Robinson Crusoe*

Robinson Crusoe *was one of the first English novels to pioneer realism in prose fiction. How is the narration realistic, and how is it unrealistic? How does it compare with what we consider realistic today?*

Examine the physical descriptions, especially those of objects or actions. How are they realistic?

Can one see these things? Is the writer's vision limited in any way (that is, does he focus on any particular area of reality to the exclusion of others)? Is the book psychologically realistic?

(II)

Daniel Defoe: *Robinson Crusoe;*
William Golding: *Pincher Martin*

Robinson Crusoe AND *Pincher Martin*

How do these two books, written hundreds of years apart, treat the same situation (abandonment on a desert island)?

Is each writer especially interested in physical or in psychological events? How are things described in the two books? What in each is realistic and unrealistic? How are they similar in theme, if at all? (II)

Daniel Defoe: *Robinson Crusoe*

THE APPEAL OF *Robinson Crusoe*

Why do you think the adventures of Robinson Crusoe have such universal appeal?

Consider Crusoe's situation. Isn't this the sort of escape that we all desire? (I)

Daniel Defoe: *Roxana*

UNITY IN *Roxana*

How is unity achieved in Roxana?

Is there unity of plot? Is the reader's interest held through subtlety of characterization or diversity of action or both? Consider the device of reoccurrence: for example, how does the Turkish dance serve to unify the novel?   (II)

Daniel Defoe: *Roxana*

THE CHARACTER OF DEFOE'S ROXANA

In terms of Christian morality, Roxana is a flagrant sinner. Yet she has her redeeming qualities. What are these qualities?

Consider her faithfulness to her various lovers, as well as her own honest self-evaluation, in your discussion.   (II)

John Dryden: "Absalom and Achitophel"

THE ALLEGORY OF "ABSALOM AND ACHITOPHEL"

Discuss the political overtones of Dryden's poem. In what way is satire generated?

Correlate the biblical story of Absalom with the political events of Dryden's era.   (II)

John Dryden: "Absalom and Achitophel"

PRIDE IN "ABSALOM AND ACHITOPHEL"

Discuss the meaning and function of pride in the poem.

Show how prideful action affects the course of the action in the poem. How is pride presented through metaphor and language? How does Dryden present his own and society's judgment of pride?   (II)

John Dryden: *Prologues and Epilogues*
DRYDEN'S STYLE

Pick one of Dryden's prologues or epilogues and try to characterize its manner and style. How does the mode of expression relate to the subject being expressed? Remember that these verses were spoken before a learned and fickle playgoing audience.

Examine allusion, diction, and syntax. Characterize the language. What is the moral attitude of the verse?   (III)

Henry Fielding: *Joseph Andrews;* Samuel Richardson: *Pamela, Clarissa*
DEFINITIONS OF VIRTUE: RICHARDSON AND FIELDING

In both Pamela *and* Clarissa, *Richardson seems to be saying that the cardinal virtue is chastity. Judging from* Joseph Andrews, *what do you think Fielding considered to be the cardinal virtue?*

Consider the people in the coach who refuse to assist the robbed and beaten Joseph. What virtue do they lack?   (II)

Henry Fielding: *Joseph Andrews*
CONTEMPT FOR THE LAW IN *Joseph Andrews*

In Joseph Andrews, *Fielding provides some social commentary. What is his attitude toward the legal system?*

Re-examine the chapter in which Joseph is brought before the judge.   (II)

Henry Fielding: *Tom Jones*
DRAMATIC ELEMENTS IN *Tom Jones*

What dramatic elements can you find in Tom Jones?

Consider the importance of the dramatic situation and of the devices of surprise discovery and mistaken identity. (I)

Henry Fielding: *Tom Jones*
THE MAGNETISM OF TOM JONES

Tom Jones is a character of considerable moral weakness. What aspect of his personality makes this weakness ultimately forgivable?

Compare Tom with Blifil. (I)

Henry Fielding: *Tom Jones*
THE MORALITY OF HENRY FIELDING

During Fielding's lifetime, Tom Jones *was condemned as an immoral book. What, do you think, is Fielding's morality?*

Consider the relationship between charity, compassion, and hypocrisy in *Tom Jones*. (II)

Samuel Johnson: *Lives of the Poets;* John Milton: "Lycidas"
JOHNSON'S CRITICISM OF "LYCIDAS"

Discuss the essential points of Samuel Johnson's criticism of "Lycidas," in his "life of Milton." Do you sympathize with Johnson's objection?

Consider other famous poems to which Johnson's criticism would be equally applicable.   (III)

Samuel Johnson: *The Rambler, The Idler*

AUTOBIOGRAPHICAL ELEMENTS IN THE WORKS OF SAMUEL JOHNSON

Can you find any evidence of self-evaluation in the writings of Dr. Johnson? Confine your study to the Moral Essays.

Consider the portrait of Sober, in the thirty-first essay from *The Idler*.   (II)

Alexander Pope, Jonathan Swift: poetry and prose

THE SATIRE OF SWIFT AND POPE

Compare the satiric techniques of Pope and Swift.

Consider the use of personae, the mock epic technique, satiric portraiture, and allegory. In a satire of Pope's, is the poet's position clear? Is this true of Swift's works?   (III)

Alexander Pope: *Essay on Criticism*

POPE THE CRITIC

Explore Pope's own canons of criticism, presented in the Essay on Criticism.

In Pope's view, what is the role of the poet in relation to his reader and in relation to nature? What is the role of the critic?   (II)

Alexander Pope: *Essay on Man;*
Jonathan Swift: *Gulliver's Travels*

THE NATURE OF MAN: POPE AND SWIFT

How do Pope and Swift differ in their evaluations of man?

In a letter to Pope, Swift accused him of being a misanthrope because he demanded perfection of mankind. How does this observation illuminate the two authors' differing conceptions of the nature of man? (II)

Alexander Pope: *The Rape of the Lock*

VIRGILIAN REFERENCES IN *The Rape of the Lock*

Explore Pope's allusions to Virgil's Aeneid *in* The Rape of the Lock.

How do these allusions help to unfold the meaning of the poem? How do they compound the satire? (III)

Alexander Pope: *The Rape of the Lock*

MOCK EPIC TECHNIQUE IN *The Rape of the Lock*

In what way and to what effect does Pope use mock epic technique in The Rape of the Lock?

How does Pope's use of the epic mode generate satire? (II)

Alexander Pope: "Windsor Forest";
Andrew Marvell: "The Garden"

NATURE IN "WINDSOR FOREST" AND "THE GARDEN"

Compare and contrast the treatments of nature in these two poems.

How does Pope, in his imagination, view the forest? How does Marvell see the garden? How do both poets deal with and exclude violence and disorder? Discuss the poets' use of language and rhythm in the course of your essay.   (II)

Samuel Richardson: *Clarissa, Pamela;* Henry Fielding: *Tom Jones*

CHARACTERIZATION IN RICHARDSON AND FIELDING

Taken as a whole, how do Richardson's characters differ from Fielding's?

Does Clarissa have any vices? Has Lovelace any virtues? Does Tom Jones have any vices? Is he to be condemned for them?   (II)

Samuel Richardson: *Pamela*

THE EPISTOLARY STYLE IN *Pamela*

Why is the epistolary style perfectly suited to Richardson's purpose in Pamela?

Consider the very nature of a letter—its intrinsic privacy, its secrecy, and its immediacy.   (II)

Samuel Richardson: *Pamela, Clarissa*

Pamela AND *Clarissa* CONTRASTED

The central conflict is the same for both Pamela and Clarissa. What is the basic difference between the two books?

One critic has called *Pamela* a bourgeois comedy and *Clarissa* a bourgeois tragedy. Do you agree?   (II)

Anthony Smollett: *Humphry Clinker*

THE EPISTOLARY STYLE IN *Humphry Clinker*

How does the use of the epistolary style broaden the reader's perspective of the events and characters in the novel?

How many points of view are expressed in *Humphry Clinker?* Compare the epistolary technique in Smollett's book with that in Richardson's *Pamela.*					(II)

Anthony Smollett: *Roderick Random*

Roderick Random: PORTRAIT OF THE ARTIST

Is there any evidence to suggest that Roderick Random *is to some extent an autobiography?*

What significance can be attached to the journey to London, the meeting with the unsuccessful playwright, and the stint in the navy?					(I)

Laurence Sterne: *A Sentimental Journey*

THE RELIGIOUS IMPLICATIONS OF SENTIMENTALITY IN *A Sentimental Journey*

Is sentimentality a mode of behavior or a moral code for Parson Yorick?

Discover how "sentimentality" and "sensibility" are described in religious terms.					(II)

Laurence Sterne: *Tristram Shandy*

NARRATIVE TECHNIQUE IN *Tristram Shandy*

What devices does Sterne use to convey to us the unique world of Tristram Shandy? How does his narrative technique foreshadow that of the psychological novel?

Discuss and illustrate Sterne's use of free association, subjective reality, shifts in time, and other techniques, which help to create the style of *Tristram Shandy*. Carefully explicate one or more passages; show how this kind of writing led to the psychological novel of the twentieth century. **(I)**

Laurence Sterne: *Tristram Shandy;* Virginia Woolf: *To the Lighthouse*

THE PSYCHOLOGICAL NOVEL: VIRGINIA WOOLF AND LAURENCE STERNE

Demonstrate how the groundwork is laid in Tristram Shandy *for the modern psychological novel. Discuss the narrative techniques used in Sterne's novel and in* To the Lighthouse, *pointing to parallels on many levels.*

Carefully examine and cite examples of the narrative devices used by the two novelists; show how Woolf is indebted to Sterne as her precursor in the genre of the psychological novel. Consider similarities in their general outlook as well.   **(II)**

Jonathan Swift: *The Battle of the Books;* Alexander Pope: *The Rape of the Lock*

The Rape of the Lock AND *The Battle of the Books*

Compare the satiric technique in Pope's The Rape of the Lock *with Swift's technique in* The Battle of the Books.

Consider the use of the mock epic technique. Is Swift's work also allegorical? Does Swift use allu-

sion to generate satire in the way that Pope does?
(I)

Jonathan Swift: *Gulliver's Travels*
THE RELATIONSHIP OF SWIFT TO GULLIVER

To what degree are we to assume that the opinions of Gulliver are the opinions of Swift?

Do we sympathize with Gulliver in the first book?
Do we sympathize with him later on, at the end of the fourth book, when he rejects mankind for the Houyhnhnms?   (II)

Jonathan Swift: *Gulliver's Travels*
CULTURAL STANDARDS IN *Gulliver's Travels*

In Gulliver, *Swift satirizes many cultural institutions. Does he offer any alternatives?*

Do any of the characters in the book seem to represent the cultural standards of which Swift approves? Consider the Brobdingnagian King (Book 3) and the Spanish sea captain (Book 4).   (II)

Jonathan Swift: *A Tale of a Tub*
A Tale of a Tub: A BOOK ABOUT BOOKS

In what way is the apparent form and style of A Tale of a Tub *a satire upon Grubstreet writing?*

A Tale of a Tub contains "An Apology," a "Postscript," a "Dedication," a note from "the Bookseller to the Reader," another "Dedication," an "Index," a "Preface," and an "Introduction."

What is Swift saying? Consider also the narrator's inability to understand figurative language in abstract terms.   (III)

Jonathan Swift: *A Tale of a Tub*

THE NARRATOR IN *A Tale of a Tub*

Who is the narrator of A Tale of a Tub?

What is the narrator's attitude toward Grub-street, modern literature, modern literary criticism, the new science?   (I)

James Thompson: "The Seasons"

THE IMPORTANCE OF "THE SEASONS"

Does Thompson's poem reflect the so-called Age of Reason, when it was written, or does it look forward to the poetry of the Romantic period?

Consider the importance of description in this poem. At the same time, how does the poem reflect the influence of Milton?   (II)

Henry Vaughan: poetry

PEACE IN THE POETRY OF VAUGHAN

Trace the recurring images of, and the many references to, peace in the poetry of Vaughan.

Study the polarity of subject matter in Vaughan's works. His poems describe either the destruction that results from estrangement with God or the peace consequent to communion with Him.   (II)

The Romantic Period (1798–1832)

William Blake: "The Tyger"; Rainer Maria Rilke: "The Panther"

BLAKE AND RILKE: A COMPARISON OF TWO POEMS

A comparison of Blake and Rilke.

Compare and contrast the two texts. Develop a theory to account for your results. (III)

William Blake: "The Lamb," "The Tyger"

"THE TYGER" AND "THE LAMB"

Compare the two poems and decide what Blake means by "innocence" and "experience."

How does the imagery of each poem express the difference between them? Which poem do you think is closer to reality? (I)

William Blake: *Songs of Innocence* and *Songs of Experience*

THE BALANCE OF OPPOSITES

A discussion of Blake's Songs of Innocence *and* Songs of Experience.

Examine the corresponding poems in the two collections. Point out the contrasts between representative pairs. Why do you think Blake uses this technique? Is he advocating either point of view wholly or does he intend to set up a dialectic? (II)

George Gordon, Lord Byron: *Don Juan*
USES OF IRONY IN *Don Juan*

Discuss the purpose and uses of irony in the poem.

How does the poet view life? Why should this lead him to use irony? How do language and rhythm express irony? (II)

Samuel Taylor Coleridge: "Dejection: An Ode," "Christabel"
"DEJECTION: AN ODE" AND "CHRISTABEL"

Relate the theme of the first poem to that of the second.

How does the concept of imagination presented in the first poem explain the theme and imagery of the second? (I)

Samuel Taylor Coleridge: "Frost at Midnight"; John Keats: "Ode on a Grecian Urn"
SILENCE IN "FROST AT MIDNIGHT" AND "ODE ON A GRECIAN URN"

A discussion of these poets' conceptions of silence.

Compare and contrast the meaning and uses of silence in these poems. (II)

Samuel Taylor Coleridge: "Kubla Khan"
IMAGINATION IN "KUBLA KHAN"

What is the poem's purpose, and how does it achieve it?
Characterize the imagery and describe its effect. Look for unity of imagery. Explain its presence or absence. (I)

Samuel Taylor Coleridge: "Kubla Khan," "Phantom or Fact"

"PHANTOM OR FACT" AND "KUBLA KHAN"

Discuss these poems in terms of the realism of pure imginary experience.

How does the imagery of each poem create a world apart from, and yet as "real" as, the everyday world? (II)

Samuel Taylor Coleridge: "Kubla Khan"; Percy Bysshe Shelley: "Ode to the West Wind"

"KUBLA KHAN" AND "ODE TO THE WEST WIND"

Compare and contrast the imaginative experience in the poems.

Discuss the imagery of each poem and relate it to theme. How is the language of each poem suited to its purpose? (III)

John Keats: "The Fall of Hyperion"; George Gordon, Lord Byron: "Manfred"

GUILT IN "THE FALL OF HYPERION" AND "MANFRED"

Compare and contrast the expression and significance of guilt in the two poems.

What is the power of guilt in each poem? How does this theme relate to the over-all meaning? What are the images of guilt? (III)

John Keats: "Hyperion"; Percy Bysshe Shelley: "Adonais"

MYTH IN "HYPERION" AND "ADONAIS"

Compare and contrast the use of mythological figures in the two poems.

Why did each poet adopt myth? How does the use of myth in each case convey the poet's meaning? How successful is each in revivifying myth? How is this done? How does it fail?   (III)

John Keats: "Hyperion"; Percy Bysshe Shelley: "Prometheus Unbound"

"HYPERION" AND "PROMETHEUS UNBOUND"

Compare and contrast theme, metaphor, and texture in these two poems.

What is the meaning of each poem? How does the poetic language relate to it in each case? Which is a greater poem, and why?   (II)

John Keats: "Ode on a Grecian Urn"; William Carlos Williams: "A Sort of a Song"

"NO IDEAS BUT IN THINGS"

An application of this quotation from William Carlos Williams to Keats' "Ode on a Grecian Urn."

Explore the way in which objective images are used to contain ideas in Keats' poem. Are the images and the ideas separable? Does Williams' poetic dictum seem to apply, or not? Why?   (II)

John Keats: "Ode on a Grecian Urn"; T. S. Eliot: *Four Quartets*

KEATS AND ELIOT: MAN'S EXISTENCE IN TIME

A comparison of Keats' "Ode on a Grecian Urn" with Eliot's Four Quartets, *with a view to establishing their respective viewpoints on the role of time and timelessness in man's existence.*

Close textual reading. Do not attempt to touch on all the points made in the *Four Quartets,* as this would be of extreme difficulty. What is the relation of time to the timeless in each? How do time and the timeless enter into the determination of the nature of truth, in each poet's view? (III)

John Keats: "Ode to a Nightingale." "Ode on a Grecian Urn"

"Ode to a Nightingale" and "Ode on a Grecian Urn"

Compare and contrast the experiences in these poems.

What leads to an escape to another sort of reality in each poem? How are these sources similar or different? (II)

John Keats: "Ode to a Nightingale"; Percy Bysshe Shelley: "To a Skylark"

"Ode to a Nightingale" and "To a Skylark"

Compare the meaning of a bird's song for Keats and for Shelley.

How does each poet treat the experience? Which poet experiences the music of the song more deeply? For which does it become more abstract? Discuss imagery and meter in making your points. (II)

John Keats: "To Autumn"; William Wordsworth: "Tinturn Abbey"

Nature in "To Autumn" and "Tinturn Abbey"

Compare and contrast the reaction to and uses of nature in these poems.

How does each poet react to nature? How does
language reflect or transform experience?   (II)

Sir Walter Scott: *Waverley*

WAVERLEY'S JOURNEY

*How would you characterize Waverley's journey
to Scotland in other than a geographical sense?
What is the meaning of the past in the novel?
How much of history is realistic and how much is
a source for romance?*

Explain Waverley's loss of personal and national
identity in terms of the journey.   (III)

Percy Bysshe Shelley: "Adonais"; John Milton: "Lycidas"

"ADONAIS" AND "LYCIDAS"

Compare and contrast these poems as elegies.

How does each poet conceptualize the problem of
death? How is death transmuted from evil to
good? Describe the method and imagery of each
poem and relate these to their approach to the
problem.   (III)

Percy Bysshe Shelley: "Adonais," "Mont Blanc," "The Sensitive Plant"

THE MICROCOSM IN SHELLEY

*Show how Shelley often uses a particular object
or locale as a symbol or microcosm of the entire
universe.*

How do Rome and the Protestant Cemetery, or
the garden, or the Vale of Chamonix represent
the universe?   (II)

Percy Bysshe Shelley: "Adonais"

THE ROLE OF VENUS IN "ADONAIS"

In the Venus and Adonis myth, Venus is the lover of Adonis. What is her (i.e., Urania's) role in Shelley's poem?

What power does Urania have? Can she be translated into Christian terms? (II)

Percy Bysshe Shelley: "Ozymandias"; William Butler Yeats: "The Second Coming"

"OZYMANDIAS" AND "THE SECOND COMING"

Compare and contrast the sense of apocalypse in these poems.

Show how theme and metaphor are related in each case. Which is more terrifying? Why? (II)

Percy Bysshe Shelley: "Speculations on Metaphysics"

THE MEANING OF REALITY IN SHELLEY

In what capacity do objects of this world gain their reality, according to Shelley?

What is the function of the mind? Does the mind "create" or "perceive"? By what means are "things" created? (II)

William Wordsworth: "It Is a Beauteous Evening"; William Blake: "To the Evening Star"

"IT IS A BEAUTEOUS EVENING" AND "TO THE EVENING STAR"

Compare and contrast imagery and theme in the two poems.

Examine theme and imagery and their relationship. How strong is the personal voice of the poet? Which expresses a greater uneasiness?   (II)

William Wordsworth: "Ode: Intimations of Immortality"

WORDSWORTH'S VIEW OF TRUTH

A discussion of the philosophical content of Wordsworth's "Ode."

How does the poet picture the process of arriving at truth? How is our present existence in time linked to timeless and eternal things?   (III)

William Wordsworth: "The Prelude"; Sir Walter Scott: *Waverley*

SCOTT AND WORDSWORTH: VIEWS ON HUMAN CONSCIOUSNESS

Compare and contrast the approaches to the human consciousness in these two works.

Consider man's reaction to nature and his power of imagination in the two works. How does man in each case regard his fellow man?   (III)

William Wordsworth: "The Prelude"; John Milton: "Lycidas"

ALLUSION IN "THE PRELUDE" AND "LYCIDAS"

Compare and contrast the types and methods of allusion in the two poems.

What is the purpose of allusion for Wordsworth and Milton? How does allusion relate to their larger purpose in their poetry? How does allusion relate to youth and growth in each? (III)

William Wordsworth: "The Prelude"

VISION IN "THE PRELUDE"

Pick a passage in "The Prelude" in which the poet's experience of nature seems to carry him into another dimension of reality.

How does the description itself convey the intensity of the experience? What is the meaning of the vision? (III)

William Wordsworth: "The Solitary Reaper," "I Wandered Lonely as a Cloud"

WORDSWORTH: TWO POEMS CONTRASTED

Compare and contrast the imagery and theme of these two poems.

How would you describe the experience in each case? Which is more important in each, the object seen or heard, or the experience of the poet's reaction? (I)

William Wordsworth, Samuel Taylor Coleridge: ballads

THE BALLADS OF WORDSWORTH AND COLERIDGE

Choose a ballad by each author and compare and contrast the two.

What is the point of the ballad for each? To what realities does the ballad bring the reader close, in each case? (II)

The Victorian Period (1832–1901)

Matthew Arnold: "Dover Beach";
Joseph Conrad: *Heart of Darkness*

"DOVER BEACH" AND *Heart of Darkness*

A discussion of common themes in the two works.

Each work is essentially a picture of a world in decay because of a state of chaos and confusion. Relate Arnold's "darkling plain/Where ignorant armies clash by night" to the evil in vacancy pictured in *Heart of Darkness*. How do the two authors treat their common themes? How do they differ?   (II)

Matthew Arnold: "The Future,"
"The Buried Life"

THEME AND METAPHOR IN "THE FUTURE" AND
    "THE BURIED LIFE"

Decide what the subjects of the poems are and how the poet deals with them.

Close textual reading.   (II)

Matthew Arnold: "Thyrsis"; John Milton:
"Lycidas"

"THYRSIS" AND "LYCIDAS"

Compare and contrast theme, metaphor, and texture in the poems.

How do these poems celebrate the memory of the dead? Discuss this in terms of metaphor, texture, rhythm, and poetic form.   (II)

Jane Austen: *Emma, Pride and Prejudice*

ELIZABETH AND EMMA: TWO AUSTENIAN HEROINES

Compare Elizabeth and Emma as heroines. How do they differ? What does this tell you about changes in Austen's view of human nature between the two novels?

How does each character treat the other characters around her? (II)

Jane Austen: *Pride and Prejudice*

LITERARY FORMS IN *Pride and Prejudice*

What literary forms, other than that of prose fiction, does Austen use in her novel? What reasons can you give for her employing them?

Examine Jane Austen's style and method of characterization. (III)

Jane Austen: *Pride and Prejudice*

THE USE OF DEAD METAPHORS IN JANE AUSTEN

An examination of how Austen uses dead metaphors, which enter unobtrusively and come to bear their original metaphorical meaning in her text.

Find as many examples as possible of dead metaphors in *Pride and Prejudice*. In each case, note the original meaning of the metaphor and show how it is applied to the themes of the novel. (III)

Jane Austen: *Pride and Prejudice;* Charles Dickens: *Bleak House*

DRAMATIC ELEMENTS IN *Pride and Prejudice* AND *Bleak House*

Compare and contrast these novels in terms of elements of plot and characterization that might be termed dramatic.

What are the traits peculiar to dramatic presentation? Which of these do Austen and Dickens use in their novels? Why might both works fail as plays?   (III)

Emily Brontë: *Wuthering Heights*

THE USE OF MULTIPLE NARRATORS IN *Wuthering Heights*

What effect is produced by the author's use of several narrators in Wuthering Heights?

Note that the narration is made up of contributions by several people. Does this add to its credibility? How do we respond to the narrators themselves? Do we believe all their accounts equally?   (II)

Elizabeth Barrett Browning: *Sonnets from the Portuguese*

IMAGERY IN *Sonnets from the Portuguese*

Discuss the use of imagery in the sonnets.

What does the poet's choice of images reveal about her preoccupations? How are these images expressed in words, rhythms, and poetic structures?
                                                        (I)

Robert Browning: "Andrea del Sarto"

AN EXAMINATION OF BROWNING'S ANDREA DEL SARTO

Decide how Browning means the reader to regard this character. Are del Sarto's reasons for failure convincing?

Close textual reading.   (II)

Robert Browning: "The Bishop Orders His Tomb at St. Praxed's Church"

BROWNING'S BISHOP: A LIKELY RENAISSANCE FIGURE?

How does Browning recreate the luxury of the prelate's Italian Renaissance world?

Examine the imagery and its effect upon the reader.   (II)

Robert Browning: "Childe Roland to the Dark Tower Came"

THE ALLEGORY OF "CHILDE ROLAND TO THE DARK TOWER CAME"

What do you think the journey signifies? Where is this "Waste Land?"

Close textual reading.   (II)

Robert Browning: "My Last Duchess"

A DISCUSSION OF BROWNING'S DUCHESS

A discussion of "My Last Duchess."

What dramatic situation is implied in "My Last Duchess"? To whom is the Duke speaking? Who is downstairs? What exactly is the story of his "last Duchess"? What kind of man is the Duke? How does Browning convey all this information without stating it outright?   (I)

Thomas Carlyle: *Sartor Resartus*

IRONY IN *Sartor Resartus*

Discuss the forms and uses of irony in the book.

What is the relationship between irony and the themes of the book?   (II)

Lewis Carroll: "Jabberwocky"

NONSENSE AND SENSE

An examination of "Jabberwocky."

Consider Humpty Dumpty's explication of "Jabberwocky," especially his remarks on portmanteau words. How does this passage clarify the poem, if at all? Is the poem meaningless? If so, does it matter? In what way is it meaningful (or communicative) even in places that do not make strict sense?   (II)

Charles Dickens: *Bleak House*

ALIENATION IN *Bleak House*

Find the sources of human loneliness in the novel. What is the ultimate cause of the separations?

Closely examine the characters and the forces outside them that affect their behavior.   (III)

Charles Dickens: *Bleak House;*
George Eliot: *The Mill on the Floss*

DICKENS TO GEORGE ELIOT: THE SHIFT IN WORLD VIEW

Discuss the basic change in the cosmic picture from Dickens to George Eliot, by comparing Dick-

ens' Bleak House *with Eliot's* The Mill on the Floss.

It has often been said that Dickens was the last English novelist to give an ordered picture of the world. Consider how he does so in *Bleak House* in terms of his use of thematic images and symbols. Then examine the breakdown of order and the radically different picture as given by George Eliot.   (III)

Charles Dickens: *Great Expectations*
PIP'S GROWTH AS A PERSON

Show how Pip changes and matures in the course of Great Expectations.

Try to formulate Pip's attitudes at the various stages of his life and the influences that help to change him. How, in particular, does he finally overcome his original snobbery?   (I)

Charles Dickens: *Our Mutual Friend*
THE RIVER IN *Our Mutual Friend*

What actual and symbolic role does the river play in Our Mutual Friend?

Note not only the physical intrusions of the river into the plot, but its use as a central symbol of the book. Examine in particular the relationship between the river and the downfall or regeneration of certain characters.   (II)

Charles Dickens: *The Pickwick Papers*
THE GRUESOME TALES IN *The Pickwick Papers*

What is the meaning of the gruesome stories told in the course of the book? How do they provide an insight into Dickens' attitude toward Pickwick and the Pickwickians?

Analyze the reactions of Pickwick and his friends to each of the tales. Try to relate these analyses to a generalization about their character.   (I)

Charles Dickens: any major work

"RECALLED TO LIFE": THE THEME OF REGENERATION IN DICKENS

One of the recurring phrases in Dickens is "recalled to life." Examine the theme of regeneration as it occurs in any of Dickens' major works (Bleak House *is an excellent choice for this topic*).

Discuss the disappearance or supposed death of persons who are later rediscovered, or characters' assuming a false identity while they are believed to be dead, or any other device by which Dickens' characters "die" and return to life. In each case, how does this regeneration tie in with their personal development and relate to the theme of the book?   (III)

George Eliot: *The Mill on the Floss;* Virginia Woolf: *To the Lighthouse*

ISOLATION IN GEORGE ELIOT AND VIRGINIA WOOLF

An examination of common themes in The Mill on the Floss *and* To the Lighthouse.

How does each novelist approach the theme of human isolation? What conclusions do they draw?

How, in each case, does the characters' isolation relate to the novelist's view of the universe? (II)

George Eliot: *Middlemarch*

THE PRESENCE OF THE AUTHOR IN *Middlemarch*

Discuss the extent and effect of the author's voice and opinions in the novel.

Why does the author intrude her own judgments into the course of the narrative? How does this affect the representation of reality? What can you tell of Eliot's temperament and personality from the novel? (II)

Thomas Hardy: *Far from the Madding Crowd;* Jane Austen: any novel(s)

AUSTEN ON HARDY

Write an Austenian review of Far from the Madding Crowd. *What would Austen have liked and disliked about Hardy's novel, and why?*

Isolate the essential characteristics of the novel for each author and from there derive critical standards for your review. (III)

Walter Pater: *Marius the Epicurean;* James Joyce: *A Portrait of the Artist as a Young Man*

RELIGIOUS ORTHODOXY IN PATER AND JOYCE

Compare and contrast the treatment of religious orthodoxy in these works.

How is religious orthodoxy presented in each of the novels? What effect does this theme have on the structure of each? (II)

Dante Gabriel Rossetti: "The Blessed Damozel"; John Keats: "The Eve of St. Agnes"

"THE BLESSED DAMOZEL" AND "THE EVE OF ST. AGNES"

Compare and contrast these two poems in terms of theme, metaphor, and texture.

Read closely to determine how language is used for the development of theme.   (III)

Algernon Charles Swinburne: "Atalanta in Calydon," "Nephelidia"

SWINBURNE'S METRICAL EFFECTS

A discussion of the use of meter in the choruses from "Atalanta in Calydon."

Comment on the form of Swinburne's versification, the effect it has in carrying the poem along, and the role it plays in the poem as a whole. For a novel approach, also consider his self-parody, "Nephelidia."   (II)

Alfred Tennyson: "The Lotus-Eaters"; Matthew Arnold: "Stanzas from the Grande Chartreuse"

THEME AND METAPHOR IN "THE LOTUS-EATERS" AND "STANZAS FROM THE GRANDE CHARTREUSE"

Decide what the subjects of the poems are and how the poets deal with them.

Close textual reading.   (II)

Alfred Tennyson: "Crossing the Bar"; Robert Browning: "Prospice"

"CROSSING THE BAR" AND "PROSPICE"

Compare and contrast theme, metaphor, and texture in these poems.

What is each poem about? How does the author of each use language and rhythm to say what he means? (I)

Alfred Tennyson: "The Triumph of Life"; John Keats: "The Fall of Hyperion"

GUILT IN "THE TRIUMPH OF LIFE" AND "THE FALL OF HYPERION"

Compare and contrast the meaning of guilt in the two poems.

What is the precise nature of the guilt in each poem? How does language and imagery reflect this theme? (II)

William Makepeace Thackeray: *Vanity Fair*

Vanity Fair: A REPRESENTATION OF REALITY

Examine Thackeray's method of character portrayal. Does it allow for all the different ways of looking at human beings? What limitations, if any, does his method impose on the reality of the novel as a whole?

Analyze the main characters. How different are they one from another? (II)

William Makepeace Thackeray: *Vanity Fair;* Thomas Hardy: *The Mayor of Casterbridge*

GUILT AND REDEMPTION IN THACKERAY AND HARDY

Compare and contrast the forms of guilt and redemption found in the novels.

What are the sources of guilt? How is redemption achieved? In which novel is guilt and/or redemption the stronger theme?   (III)

The Twentieth Century (1890–present)

W. H. Auden: *As He Is*
AUDEN'S ESSAY ON MAN

A discussion of the philosophy of W. H. Auden's As He Is.

Consider *As He Is* as a general statement about the human condition and attempt to formulate its content.   (II)

Joseph Conrad: *Heart of Darkness*
EVIL IN VACANCY

A discussion of the nature of evil as seen in Heart of Darkness.

The source of evil in this story is not a principle, but a void, which is far larger than Kurtz and which allows his existence. Discuss.   (II)

T. S. Eliot: *The Hollow Men;*
Joseph Conrad: *Heart of Darkness*
"MISTAH KURTZ, HE DEAD"

A comparison of The Hollow Men *and* Heart of Darkness.

Discuss the common themes in the two works. In each case, the source of evil is in hollowness or vacancy. How do the two authors treat this idea?
                              (II)

T. S. Eliot: *The Waste Land*

THE NATURE OF THE JOURNEY IN *The Waste Land*

Describe the nature of the journey, actual and metaphysical, in this poem.

Examine the theme in terms of metaphor and texture. (III)

T. S. Eliot: *The Love Song of J. Alfred Prufrock*

IMAGE AND IDEA IN "PRUFROCK"

An analysis of the relationship between the style (the images and comparisons employed) and the literal content of The Love Song of J. Alfred Prufrock.

Closely examine the means by which Eliot conveys the literal meaning in *Prufrock*. Are the images and ideas separable, or do they essentially fuse into one phenomenon? (II)

E. M. Forster: *Howard's End*

MORAL EXCELLENCE IN *Howard's End*

Discuss the standards of moral excellence in the novel and show how they are met or missed.

Examine the social behavior of each character and determine its value. What are the snares in the path of moral behavior in the book? (III)

Gerard Manley Hopkins: "God's Grandeur"

LINGUISTIC EFFECTS IN "GOD'S GRANDEUR"

An examination of Hopkins' innovations in language in the poem "God's Grandeur."

Consider Hopkins' diction, particularly his choice of verbs; his use of alliteration and assonance; and his manipulation of meter. What effects does he achieve by these techniques?   (II)

James Joyce: *A Portrait of the Artist as a Young Man*

EPIPHANY IN *A Portrait of the Artist as a Young Man*

A study of the function of revelatory moments in Joyce's novel.

What is an epiphany? Derive your illustrations from the text in explaining what an epiphany is. How do these moments function in the book? What effects do they have on Stephen's character? Does Joyce use them as a part of technique in itself? Is he successful?   (II)

James Joyce: "The Dead"

JOYCE'S PROSE STYLE IN "THE DEAD"

A discussion of Joyce's style in this story.

In the final pages of "The Dead," Joyce rises to a height of style surpassing anything else in *Dubliners*. How does his style work in these pages? Are there poetic elements in it? How does he use images? the rhythm of words? assonance and alliteration? How does the passage effect you? (II)

D. H. Lawrence: short stories

WILL AND ACTION: A BASIC PARADOX IN THE STORIES OF D. H. LAWRENCE

Analyze the difference between the thoughts and ideal actions of the characters in Lawrence's short stories and their real acts and speech.

Study the insight that Lawrence gives you into his characters. How do their actions differ from their intent? Consider also the actions that these characters take without suspecting their own motives. (II)

Harold Pinter: *The Caretaker, The Dumbwaiter*

PINTER'S USE OF EVERYDAY SPEECH

Many playwrights have great difficulty in making their dialogue sound true to life. Is this true of Pinter?

Consider Pinter's dialogue. How realistic is it? Does any of it deviate from everyday speech, and, if so, how? (II)

George Bernard Shaw: *Heartbreak House;* F. Scott Fitzgerald: *The Great Gatsby*

TWO HOUSES

A comparison of Heartbreak House *and* The Great Gatsby.

Each of these works offers a picture of a decaying society. How are they similar in theme? Do they reach similar conclusions? What characteristics seem to be peculiar to America, and which to England? Can the two viewpoints be combined? (II)

George Bernard Shaw: *Man and Superman*

SHAW AND DON JUAN

An analysis of the Shavian treatment of the Don Juan story.

Consider Shaw's handling of his material. Note what he has altered and what he has preserved and determine the significance of these changes.

(III)

George Bernard Shaw: *The Devil's Disciple, St. Joan, Major Barbara*

THE MORALITY OF GEORGE BERNARD SHAW

What is Shaw's moral doctrine?

Determine whether or not Shaw approved of the moral position exemplified by various characters in these plays. The Shavian morality is complicated and far-reaching: do not be fooled by the seemingly unshakable positions of certain characters.

(I)

John Synge: *The Playboy of the Western World*

IRISH FAMILY LIFE IN SYNGE

Analysis of the role of the family in The Playboy of the Western World.

Determine what use Synge makes of family life in the plot and theme of *The Playboy*. Does he take liberties with reality? Where? Why?

(II)

Dylan Thomas: "The Force That Through the Green Fuse Drives the Flower"; Gerard Manley Hopkins: "Spring"

THE POETIC EXPERIENCE: HOPKINS AND THOMAS

Compare and contrast the experiences presented in these poems.

Discuss the experience in each case in the light of its poetic expression through metaphor, use of language, and form. (III)

J. R. R. Tolkien: *The Lord of the Rings;* Snorri Sturluson: *Prose Edda; The Shorter Sibyl's Version*

SOURCES OF *The Lord of the Rings*

Tabulation and analysis of the sources of Tolkien's trilogy.

Read *The Lord of the Rings,* paying particular attention to the names, characters, and poems. Determine linguistic and literary sources for as many of these as necessary to support your theory of why Tolkien uses them in the way that he does. The main problem is to trace Sturluson's sources. Investigate Celtic, the Old Scandinavian tongues, and Anglo-Saxon. (III)

Virginia Woolf: "The Mark on the Wall"

STORY WITHOUT A PLOT: "THE MARK ON THE WALL"

How does this story by Virginia Woolf succeed in holding your interest in spite of its almost complete lack of external events?

Almost nothing happens in this story outwardly; but what does take place? Is there any sort of development? Is the language itself a source of interest? Is the story a "mood piece?" (II)

Virginia Woolf: *To the Lighthouse*

THE PROBLEM OF STRUCTURE IN *To the Lighthouse*

Why is the book divided into three sections?

Consider the themes explored in the book: are they finally resolved, or can they be resolved? How does the last section relate to the first? Do you think the book should be classified as a novel?

(III)

William Butler Yeats: "A Prayer for My Daughter"; Ben Jonson: "To Penshurst"

YEATS AND JONSON: SOCIAL IDEALS IN TWO ERAS

A comparison of two poems by Yeats and Ben Jonson.

How does each poet define his conception of what is ideal for society? What are the similarities and differences between the poems? Do they resemble one another in form in any way?

(II)

William Butler Yeats: "Lapis Lazuli"

"LAPIS LAZULI": THE QUALITY OF GAIETY

Discuss the meaning of the quality of gaiety in the poem.

What does Yeats mean by "gaiety"? Why is such a quality necessary? Discuss this theme in terms of metaphor and poetic structure.

(III)

AMERICAN LITERATURE

The Colonial Period Through the Nineteenth Century

Henry Adams: *The Education of Henry Adams*

THE TURNING OF THE TWENTIETH CENTURY: *The Education of Henry Adams*

The paper should deal with the great changes in intellectual attitudes in the latter half of the nineteenth century as reflected in The Education of Henry Adams: *in particular, the move away from unity and toward multiplicity.*

Attempt to characterize the intellectual climate of Adams' early life as contrasted with that of his later years. How does he view his own time and the time to come? What is meant by "education"? Refer in your discussion to similar trends in literature of the same period. (III)

James Fenimore Cooper: *The Leatherstocking Tales*

NATTY BUMPPO AS AN EPIC HERO

The Leatherstocking Tales *has been described as an epic. If this is so, then surely Natty Bumppo is an epic hero. Show how Cooper creates the heroic attributes of Natty, including his extraordinary prowess and wisdom.*

Trace the development of Natty Bumppo in *The Leatherstocking Tales*. To what degree does he change? (An analysis of the death of Natty in *The Prairie* will provide an excellent illustration of the stature and dignity of this character.) (II)

Stephen Crane: *The Red Badge of Courage*

REALISM IN *The Red Badge of Courage*

The Red Badge of Courage *is filled with direct, concrete descriptions; yet, is the book essentially realistic?*

Examine Crane's technique of describing people and events. Is the final effect realistic? Is the realism objective or subjective? Analyze specific passages in your discussion. (II)

Stephen Crane: "The Bridge"
THE USE OF THE JOURNEY IN "THE BRIDGE"

Describe the nature of the journey, actual and metaphysical, in this poem.

Examine the theme as expressed by means of metaphor and texture. (III)

Ralph Waldo Emerson: *Self-Reliance*
EMERSON AND MODERN SOCIAL CONFLICT

Analyze the moral precepts advocated in the essay Self-Reliance *in terms of their application to one or more areas of modern social reform.*

Apply the dichotomy that Emerson sees between traditional and independent outlooks and morality to an area that is at present in flux, such as racial or sexual reforms. (II)

Ralph Waldo Emerson: *Self-Reliance;* Henry David Thoreau: *Civil Disobedience*
Self-Reliance AND *Civil Disobedience*

Compare the lessons presented by these two essays.

How does each author see the relation of the individual to the laws that must govern him? (I)

Bret Harte: short stories
THE NASCENT REALISM OF BRET HARTE

Study Harte's stories as precursors to the realistic movement in American literature.

How do Harte's visions of the frontier differ from those of previous writers? How does the frontier become a stage for a realistic portrayal of characters and their fortunes? To what extent does Harte romanticize either setting or character?

(II)

Nathaniel Hawthorne: *The Scarlet Letter*

The Scarlet Letter: A STUDY OF SIN

Study the possibility that, in The Scarlet Letter, *Hawthorne is showing sin to be transgression, not against God, but against man.*

It has been observed that Hawthorne sees sin as resulting in isolation. Consider the idea that isolation may result in sin. Study the different courses of action followed by Hester and Dimmesdale. How is Hester able to reconcile herself to her guilt and recover a role in the world? Does Dimmesdale ever succeed in doing this? What would be the modern existentialist view of such a concept of sin? (III)

Nathaniel Hawthorne: "Ethan Brand"; Herman Melville: *Moby Dick*

ETHAN BRAND AND CAPTAIN AHAB

Compare the characters and actions of Ahab and Ethan Brand in terms of the morality that each accepts.

What is the nature of Brand's quest? How is he thus cut off from other men? In what way do the answers to these questions apply to Ahab? To what degree is the choice of each man a conscious one? (II)

Nathaniel Hawthorne: prose works

HAWTHORNE AS A SYMBOLIST

Show how symbolism in Hawthorne's writings, rather than being a literary device, becomes an organic part of his perception of truth.

Analyze one or more works in which Hawthorne's prose reaches a clearly symbolic level. How are the symbols keys to understanding? How is the symbolic writing of Hawthorne related to the perceptions of the Transcendentalists?   (III)

Nathaniel Hawthorne: *Twice-Told Tales*

THE PATHETIC FALLACY IN *Twice-Told Tales*

Discuss Hawthorne's consistent attribution of a sympathetic quality to the setting in his short stories.

Choose several stories in which descriptions of settings figure importantly. How does the setting in each case seem to parallel or even determine the mood of the action?   (I)

Washington Irving: *The Legend of Sleepy Hollow*

THE CHARACTER OF ICHABOD CRANE

What sort of character is Ichabod Crane? Why is his being tricked by Brom Bones inevitable?

How does Irving describe Ichabod? What makes him a ridiculous character? What is implied by the change in Ichabod's character after his flight from the Horseman?   (I)

Henry Wadsworth Longfellow: poetry

MYTHOLOGICAL AND LEGENDARY ALLUSIONS IN
LONGFELLOW

*Study Longfellow's use of myth and legend in his
poetry.*

Consider representative examples of Longfellow's
poetry. How is his use of mythological allusions
compatible with the diction and attitude of the
poems? Do these allusions add greater depth to the
poems, or do they serve merely as ornamentation?
(I)

Robert Lowell, T. S. Eliot: poetry

VIEWS OF REALITY: LOWELL AND ELIOT

*Choose a poem by each author; compare and con-
trast them in terms of the poets' views of reality.*

Examine all aspects of the treatment of the theme
in each poem, including use of language and poetic
form. (III)

Herman Melville: *Moby Dick;*
The Book of Job

AHAB AND JOB CONTRASTED

*Compare the sufferings, the actions, and the fate
of Job with those of Ahab.*

How may the loss of Ahab's leg be compared with
the apparently causeless punishment of Job?
Show how both contemplate striking out at that
which has afflicted them. How are Job's final decision and his fate related to those of Ahab? (III)

Herman Melville: *Moby Dick*

THE RIDDLE OF THE WHALE

Study the symbolism of Moby Dick.

Discuss the various ideas that the white whale has been interpreted to represent. Do you favor any one of these interpretations? What evidence supports them?   (III)

Herman Melville: *Billy Budd*

MORAL AND ETHICAL CONFLICTS IN *Billy Budd*

What moral and ethical conclusions can be drawn from Billy Budd?

What are the moral and ethical conflicts in the story? What reasons are advanced on either side in the final decision about Billy? How are opposing arguments resolved? Do you think the verdict is just? why?   (I)

Herman Melville: *Bartleby the Scrivener*

THE DISSENTER IN AMERICAN SOCIETY: *Bartleby the Scrivener*

Discuss Bartleby's unwillingness to adhere to standards of behavior that he does not accept and his resulting isolation from society.

What attitude characterizes Bartleby? What is his characteristic expression? How is his dissension rewarded?   (II)

Edgar Allen Poe: "The Fall of the House of Usher"

GOTHIC ELEMENTS IN "THE FALL OF THE HOUSE OF USHER"

Although "The Fall of the House of Usher" is an allegory, it is also an excellent example of the gothic technique for which Poe is famous. Show how, in this story, Poe creates a grotesque and supernatural world.

Discuss the setting and mood of the story: how do they enhance the elements of the plot? Why does the presence of the narrator, and his attitude, add to the horror and suspense? Roderick is aware of his coming doom: why is this more effective than if he had been ignorant of it? **(I)**

Edgar Allen Poe: *The Narrative of Arthur Gordon Pym*

ADVENTURE AND ALLEGORY: *The Narrative of Arthur Gordon Pym*

Almost from beginning to end, this book is a record of a journey to incredible places; at the end, it becomes an allegory. Study this transition and try to determine why Poe wrote the Narrative *in this way.*

What effect do Pym's travels prior to his arrival in Tsalaal create on the reader? At what point does it become clear that Poe has introduced allegorical overtones? What meaning can you suggest for the "Incredible Adventures" in the South? **(II)**

Henry David Thoreau: *Walden;* Walt Whitman: *Leaves of Grass*

THOREAU AND WHITMAN CONTRASTED

Although Thoreau respected Whitman as a poet, there are basic differences in their outlooks. Draw this contrast.

Compare Thoreau's feelings regarding his fellow men's modes of living with Whitman's celebration of the various aspects of American life. How does Whitman's sensuality compare with Thoreau's attitude?   (II)

Henry David Thoreau: *Walden*
THE THEME OF REBIRTH IN *Walden*

Demonstrate the rebirth theme as being central to the philosophy of Walden.

Study rebirth and regeneration as lessons to be derived from Nature in *Walden*. In what way are many of Thoreau's concerns connected with this theme? How is the structure of *Walden* further demonstrative of this theme?   (I)

Mark Twain: *The Adventures of Tom Sawyer;* Sherwood Anderson: *Winesburg, Ohio*
TOM SAWYER AND GEORGE WILLARD

A comparison of Tom Sawyer and George Willard of Winesburg, Ohio. *In each case, the book is the story of an American boyhood; how do they differ?*

Consider the narrative technique, the author's intention, the tone and atmosphere of each book. How do the authors' ideas differ? How has the conception of "an American boyhood" changed in the years between the publication of these two books?   (II)

Mark Twain: *The Adventures of Huckleberry Finn;* J. D. Salinger: *The Catcher in the Rye*
HUCKLEBERRY FINN TO HOLDEN CAULFIELD

A comparison of these two stories of adolescence in America.

How have the attitudes and values of the young changed since the time of Mark Twain? How has the psychological atmosphere surrounding adolescence changed? Have the two stories any elements in common? How do the authors' intentions compare? Which book seems to you to be more successful?   (I)

Walt Whitman: *Leaves of Grass*

THE WANDERING OF THE SPIRIT: *Leaves of Grass*

Show how Whitman's poetry centers around the theme of the division and reintegration of the spirit.

Study such poems as "Song of · Myself," "The Sleepers," and "As I Ebb'd with the Ocean of Life." In what way are these poems expressions of a search to unite the spirit?   (II)

John Winthrop: *A Model of Christian Charity, Speech to the General Court;* John Cotton: *Limitation of Government, Christian Calling*

PURITANISM AND THE INDIVIDUAL OUTLOOK: JOHN WINTHROP AND JOHN COTTON

Keeping in mind that both these authors are bound by the Puritan ethic, demonstrate the basic differences in their views of man and his relation to God.

Study several essays by Winthrop and Cotton on Christian behavior. Determine the attitude of each toward mankind and toward God's position in morality. To what extent are the authors' feelings rooted in their role in the community?   (II)

The Twentieth Century

Edward Albee: *The American Dream*

SATIRE IN *The American Dream*

A discussion of Albee's The American Dream.

The dialogue and characterization in *The American Dream* are far from realistic. How does Albee use the freedom of fantasy to create satire? How does he deflate and invert accepted values, and to what effect?   (II)

Sherwood Anderson: *Winesburg, Ohio*

Winesburg, Ohio AS A *Bildungsroman*

In what ways can Winesburg, Ohio *be considered a* Bildungsroman *(a story of growing up) about George Willard? Consider how the book illuminates his character and development.*

A chronological portrait of George Willard may be extracted from the book. Is the book, then, mainly concerned with his growing up? or is he rather the connecting character in a series of separate stories? Carefully explicate Anderson's narrative technique.   (II)

E. E. Cummings: "Buffalo Bill's"

CUMMINGS' USE OF LANGUAGE: "BUFFALO BILL'S"

A discussion of the linguistic devices in one of Cummings' poems.

Concentrate on the poet's choice of words and on his typographical innovations: how does his use of language and form affect the reader? (II)

John Dos Passos: *U.S.A.*

AMERICA IN FOCUS: THE STYLISTIC DEVICES OF JOHN DOS PASSOS

Discuss the devices used by Dos Passos in the novel and the effect that they create.

How do the "Newsreels," "The Camera Eye," and the inserted headlines relate the events of the plot to events or situations of national significance? Discuss the ironic aspect of these sections. (II)

Richard Eberhart: "The Fury of Aerial Bombardment"

POETICAL BALANCE: "THE FURY OF AERIAL BOMBARDMENT"

A discussion of a poem by Richard Eberhart.

Notice that the last stanza of the poem is drastically different from the first three. What is the difference in terms of tone? of scope? How does this change affect the reader? Does the last stanza balance the first stanzas, and do the two parts work together? Would either part be effective without the other? (I)

William Faulkner: *Absalom, Absalom!*

Absalom, Absalom! AS A PARABLE OF THE SOUTH

In what ways does the study of Thomas Sutpen parallel the historical development of the South?

*If this book is Faulkner's statement on the South,
what is that statement?*

Examine Sutpen's career as it elucidates the ori-
gins of the southern aristocracy and the slave system, as well as the motivations behind the attitudes of present-day southerners (e.g., Quentin)
toward their country. Try to formulate a statement of Faulkner's feelings about the South—the
whites, the Negroes, and their relationship.   (I)

William Faulkner: *The Sound and the Fury*

THE WATCH WITHOUT HANDS

A study of time in Quentin's section of The Sound
and the Fury.

After the breaking of the watch in the opening
scene, there is an increasing concern with time
throughout the second section of *The Sound and
the Fury*. What thoughts does Quentin have about
time? Does it stop for him? How is his personal
time distorted? What other events having to do
with time take place?   (III)

William Faulkner: *As I Lay Dying*

THE ROLE OF ANSE BUNDREN

Anse Bundren in As I Lay Dying *may be regarded
either as a villain or as a Falstaffian comic character. What arguments can you present for your
view of the case?*

Examine Anse Bundren's part in bringing about
the events of the books and his influence on the
rest of the family (during the time prior to Ad-

die's death, as well). Should the blame for the many catastrophes that occur in the book be placed upon Anse? or is he a victim, even a comic bumbler, like the others?   (III)

William Faulkner: *Go Down, Moses,* other works

THE IMPORTANCE OF THE LAND IN FAULKNER

In Faulkner's works, the land itself embodies many positive qualities and is central to his thought. Examine Go Down, Moses, *especially in the context of his other work, and attempt to define Faulkner's feelings about the land and what he sees taking place there: specifically, how are these qualities steadily disappearing?*

In *Go Down, Moses,* analyze the story of Ike McCaslin, with a view to defining Faulkner's feelings about the land itself and the increasing mechanization of the twentieth century.   (I)

William Faulkner: *The Hamlet, The Town, The Mansion*

THE RISE OF THE SNOPESES

How does the Snopes clan, led by Flem, come to dominate the Yoknapatawpha community in the course of the trilogy? What does the story of the Snopeses reflect about Faulkner's view of the South?

Carefully examine how the Snopeses gain control over Frenchman's Bend and Jefferson: their means of taking over, the circumstances that make it possible, and the results. What is the

Snopes psychology? How do they differ from the controlling families of earlier times? Explain the nature of the drastic social change exemplified by the Snopeses.   (II)

Lawrence Ferlinghetti: "Ode to Coit Tower"; Gregory Corso: "Bombdeath"

"ODE TO COIT TOWER" AND "BOMBDEATH"

A study of the use of images by the Beat poets.

Compare and contrast the two poems. The way in which these poets use imagery is very closely linked with the Beat philosophy. Develop a theory that accounts for the patterns you detect.   (II)

F. Scott Fitzgerald: *The Great Gatsby;* Nathanael West: *The Day of the Locust*

TWO PORTRAITS OF AMERICAN SOCIETY: FITZ-
    GERALD AND WEST

A comparison of The Great Gatsby *and* The Day of the Locust.

Each of these works represents a picture of American society. What themes or conclusions do they have in common? How do they compare in technique? How do they differ? How does each author use his protagonist?   (II)

Robert Frost: "Directive"

THE USE OF THE JOURNEY IN "DIRECTIVE"

Describe the nature of the journey, actual and metaphysical, in this poem.

Examine the theme in terms of metaphor and texture.   (III)

Robert Frost: "The Death of the Hired Man"; William Wordsworth: "Michael"

TWO POEMS IN THE COMMON SPEECH

A comparison of Wordsworth's "Michael" and Frost's "The Death of the Hired Man."

Both of these poems are distinguished by their having been written in language very close to the vernacular of their times. How effective is this language in each case? Is one of the poems more artistically successful than the other? Why? (II)

Robert Frost: "Stopping by Woods on a Snowy Evening"

IMPLICATIONS

A discussion of Frost's "Stopping by Woods on a Snowy Evening."

We can learn a great deal about the man in the poem from what is only implied by the poet. What can we discover about his habits? his way of life? the place in which he lives? How does he feel about the woods? Are his feelings explicitly stated? There is a sort of conversation that takes place between the man, the horse, and the landscape. What do they say to each other? What is implied by the last stanza and particularly by the last line? (I)

Ernest Hemingway: novels

EXISTENTIALIST INFLUENCES IN HEMINGWAY

Relate the writings of Hemingway to the body of Existentialist thought.

How do Hemingway's heroes view life and death? Do they live with hope or only with courage? Compare a Hemingway hero with one of Camus'. (II)

Henry James: *The Wings of the Dove, Washington Square*

Washington Square AND *The Wings of the Dove*

A comparison of these two James novels, one early and one late, to show his development over the span of his career.

Notice that the central characters, Milly and Catherine, show many similarities and come to fairly similar ends. Show how a difference in technique and a much fuller conception of his themes on James's part differentiates *The Wings of the Dove* so sharply from *Washington Square*. Compare the style, the use of symbolism, and the scope of the two works. Could *Washington Square* have been as large a book as *Wings of the Dove* if James had written it late in his career?   (III)

Henry James: *The Art of Fiction;* William Dean Howells: *Criticism and Fiction*

HOWELLS AND JAMES: ATTITUDES TOWARD THE NOVEL

How do Howells and James differ in their beliefs as to the technique and purpose of the novel?

A careful comparison of the main points of Howells' *Criticism and Fiction* and James's *The Art of Fiction*. (James's prefaces to his novels could also be considered.) Which point of view seems to have endured better in recent fiction? It could also be fruitful to relate their criteria to their own work and each other's work.   (III)

Archibald MacLeish: "Ars Poetica"

MEANINGFUL PARADOXES

An explication of MacLeish's poem "Ars Poetica."

The poem consists almost entirely of apparently contradictory statements. How are these statements meaningful? How do the apparent contradictions resolve? What does the poem say about the art of poetry? (II)

Arthur Miller: *Death of a Salesman*

Death of a Salesman: THE AMERICAN TRAGEDY?

Is Death of a Salesman *a tragedy?*

Compare *Death of a Salesman* with examples of Shakespearean and classical tragedy in an attempt to decide for yourself whether or not it is a full-fledged tragic work. (This question has been the subject of much controversy.) (II)

Frank Norris: *McTeague*

SYMBOLISM IN *McTeague*

How does Norris use symbolic elements in conveying the themes of McTeague?

Examine the text closely for actions or objects that seem to have more than a literal meaning. Consider, for example, the symbolic use of the huge gold tooth and the allusions to the color gold throughout the book. (II)

Eugene O'Neill: *Long Day's Journey into Night*

EDMUND TYRONE'S PURGATION

A discussion of Long Day's Journey into Night.

How do all the conflicts and revelations of the play act on Edmund? Is he the focus of the play? How is he changed by it? How are the past conflicts of the Tyrone family resolved in the course of the play? It has been said that Edmund emerges as the voice of all the Tyrones. Do you think this is true? Why?   (II)

Eugene O'Neill: *Mourning Becomes Electra*

O'NEILL ON *Mourning Becomes Electra*

"Masks were called for in one draft . . . but the classical connection was too insistent. Masks in that connection demand great language to speak— which let me out of it with a sickening bump! So I had to discard them. There was a realistic New England insistence in my mind, too, which would have barred great language, an insistence of the clotted and clogged and inarticulate."

Does the playwright succeed in his intention, and does his comment help towards an understanding of the play?   (II)

J. D. Salinger: "Just Before the War with the Eskimos"

STORY WITHOUT A PLOT

A discussion of how Salinger's story "Just Before the War with the Eskimos" functions in the absence of an actual plot.

What keeps up our interest in this story in spite of the fact that the external events of it are very prosaic? Does anything happen to the characters in the course of the story? Is there any development? Is it a mood or atmosphere piece? Is it possible to read anything into the story? Do you consider it a success? Why? (I)

Wallace Stevens: "Sunday Morning"

AN EXPLICATION OF "SUNDAY MORNING," BY WALLACE STEVENS

What is the literal meaning of the poem "Sunday Morning"? How do the metaphors and images work together to produce that meaning? How do traditional religious elements undergo a radical transformation in the poem?

Examine the thematic images of the poem, the use of traditional religious images, and the symbolism employed by Stevens. Do not hesitate to interpret any statement on its most evident level in attempting to ascertain the literal meaning of the poem. (III)

Wallace Stevens: "Thirteen Ways of Looking at a Blackbird"

A POEM OF IMPLICATIONS

A discussion of Stevens' poem "Thirteen Ways of Looking at a Blackbird."

How many ways does Stevens use the blackbird in this poem? What could the blackbird stand for? Does it seem to mean one thing only, or many? How do you derive meaning from the poem (since it is, on the whole, rather cryptic)? (II)

Robert Penn Warren: *The Cave;* Plato: *The Republic*

The Cave AS A PLATONIC ALLEGORY

A study of Warren's novel in terms of Plato's allegory of the cave (in The Republic).

Read Plato's comparison of human life to the cave. In what ways is this allegory carried out in Warren's novel? If it applies, how does it relate to the themes of the novel? (II)

Evelyn Waugh: *Decline and Fall*

IRONY IN *Decline and Fall*

Exploration of the many uses of irony in Evelyn Waugh's Decline and Fall.

Show how Waugh achieves his many ironic effects in statement and action. (II)

Nathanael West: *Miss Lonelyhearts;* T. S. Eliot: *The Waste Land*

Miss Lonelyhearts AND *The Waste Land*

A comparison of these two works by Nathanael West and T. S. Eliot.

Both of these works present a picture of a decaying world. In what way are these world-pictures similar? What themes do they have in common? What (if anything) do these two authors suggest about a way out of the present condition? How do the suggestions compare? (III)

Thornton Wilder: *Our Town*, other plays

THORNTON WILDER AND THE ORIENTAL THEATRE

Investigate the devices of the Oriental theatre.

Examine the structure of Wilder's work closely. Compare and contrast the unconventional devices that he uses with the conventions of the Oriental theatre. (II)

William Carlos Williams: "The Botticellian Trees"
VISUAL POETRY

A discussion of Williams' poem "The Botticellian Trees."

Read Williams' remarks on visual poetry and comment on how this view is exemplified by "The Botticellian Trees." What is Williams' technique in the poem? What aspects of poetry does he concentrate on? (II)

Thomas Wolfe: *Look Homeward, Angel, Of Time and the River, The Web and the Rock, You Can't Go Home Again*
THE STRUGGLE OF THE ARTIST: THOMAS WOLFE

Show how the major novels of Wolfe present the struggle of an artistic spirit to become reconciled with the banalities of human life.

What is the motivation of the protagonist's wanderings? What is the "blackness" which he discovers in himself? How are the characters whom he encounters representative of these conflicting forces? Is Wolfe's struggle ever reconciled? (II)

Thomas Wolfe: The Gant and Webber novels; James Joyce: The Dedalus trilogy; Nikos Kazantzakis: *Report to Greco*
THE EARTHBOUND ARTIST IN MODERN LITERATURE

Study the theme of the artist's search to reconcile his spirit with the roots of his existence in the community of mankind.

Study the writings of Wolfe, Joyce, and Kazant-
zakis. How is this theme central in their works?
In what way has much of modern literature become the relation of the artist's struggle rather
than his study of other lives? What common representations, such as the dichotomy represented
by mother and father, does this quest assume in
the works of these writers?   (III)

CLASSICAL LITERATURE

Greek and Roman

Aeschylus: *Agamemnon;* **John Webster:**
The White Devil

MARRIAGE IN *Agamemnon* AND *The White Devil*

*Compare and contrast the treatment of marriage
in the two plays.*

How does each author regard marriage? How does
marriage affect the dramatic action? What do the
characters themselves think of marriage?   (I)

Aeschylus: *Oresteia*

CONCEPTS OF JUSTICE IN THE *Oresteia*

*Discuss the evolution of the idea of justice in the
Oresteia.*

Analyze the different concepts of justice presented
in the three parts of Aeschylus' trilogy.   (I)

Aristophanes: *The Clouds;*
Molière: *The Misanthrope*

ECCENTRICITY IN *The Clouds* AND *The Misanthrope*

Compare and contrast the comic portrayals of eccentric behavior in the two plays.

What methods do the authors use to treat eccentric behavior in a comic fashion? (I)

Homer: *Odyssey;* Virgil: *Aeneid*

THE VOYAGE IN THE *Odyssey* AND THE *Aeneid*

Compare and contrast the meaning of the voyage in the Odyssey *and the* Aeneid.

In each case, what does the journey signify? How willing are the voyageurs? What do their experiences teach them? What is the ultimate object of the journey? (II)

Homer: *Iliad;* John Milton: *Paradise Lost*

DEITY IN HOMER AND MILTON

Compare and contrast the Zeus of the Iliad *with God in* Paradise Lost.

How is the deity related to man in each case? What control do they exercise over events? Discuss any other differences or similarities between the two portrayals of the deity. (II)

Thucydides: *The Peloponnesian War*

THUCYDIDES' PHILOSOPHY OF HISTORY

What is Thucydides' conception of history?

Consider how Thucydides treats his subject. What does he include? What does he omit? Why? Can historical writing be considered literature? (II)

EUROPEAN LITERATURE

Samuel Beckett: plays

THE PROBLEM OF MEANING IN BECKETT

A discussion of the meaning of Beckett's plays.

Should we consider it imperative that Beckett's work be meaningful? Is it intended to be so throughout? If it is meaningless in parts, does that meaninglessness function in a meaningful way?   (II)

Samuel Beckett: *Waiting for Godot;* Eugène Ionesco: *Rhinoceros*

WHAT IS THE ABSURD?

What is meant by the term "Theatre of the Absurd"?

Examine the basic Absurd texts. What are their common characteristics? Expound in your own words the Absurdist position.   (I)

Giovanni Boccaccio: *The Decameron*

BOCCACCIO'S MORALITY

Pick one or two of the stories in The Decameron *that deal with some kind of misbehavior. How does the story reveal Boccaccio's moral position?*

Look for a double-faced irony.   (I)

Bertolt Brecht: *A Man Is a Man, The Measures Taken*

BRECHT AND THE ORGANIZATION

An investigation of Brecht's attitude toward large, authoritative organizations.

Several of Brecht's plays deal with large organizations. How does Brecht regard them? How do his attitudes change, and what is the determining factor in that change?   (II)

Bertolt Brecht: *The Good Woman of Setzuan, The Caucasian Chalk Circle;*
William Butler Yeats: *At the Hawk's Well, The Death of Cuchulain*

THE INFLUENCE OF ORIENTAL DRAMA ON BRECHT
AND YEATS

Examine Oriental dramatic techniques employed by Brecht and Yeats.

Both Brecht and Yeats studied the Oriental drama, but for different ends. Yeats wanted a means to a personal statement, aristocratic and symbolic. Brecht's intentions were social and propagandistic, and he consequently studied Oriental stories and the refinement and clarity of Chinese acting as a means of representing, rather than enacting, emotion.   (II)

Albert Camus: *The Rebel*

CAMUS ON DUMAS *fils*

Discuss Camus' criticism of Dumas fils.

Analyze Camus' opinion of Dumas *fils* and suggest why he feels this way.   (II)

Albert Camus: *The Stranger*

ISOLATION OF THE INDIVIDUAL IN *The Stranger*

Discuss the theme of isolation in The Stranger.

What is Camus' philosophy about the individual?
How does he present his theme?   (I)

Anton Chekhov: *The Cherry Orchard*

THE TURNING POINT IN *The Cherry Orchard*

A careful explanation of where and how the turning point comes in the course of the gradual disintegration that takes place during the play.

Formulate a definition of a "turning point" in dramatic action. Then, by examining the careers of all the main characters in the play, establish where you believe the turning point of the play occurs, and why.   (III)

Pierre Corneille: *Le Cid;* Jean Baptiste Racine: *Andromaque*

THE HEROIC IDEAL

Discussion of the heroic ideal as conceived by Corneille and Racine.

What is each playwright's conception of the heroic ideal? What is the attitude of each toward mankind?   (II)

Fyodor Dostoevski: *Crime and Punishment*

THE LAZARUS MYTH IN *Crime and Punishment*

Show the recurrence of the Lazarus theme in Dostoevski's novel, and discuss its central importance to the book's theme.

In what way can Raskolnikoff be compared with Lazarus? Note Dostoevski's description of Raskolnikoff's room as a "tomb." What is the author's comment on the reformation of this character?

(II)

Fyodor Dostoevski: *The Brothers Karamazov*

THE ASSASSINATION OF GOD

A discussion of the "assassination of God" in The Brothers Karamazov.

Analyze the attitudes of the brothers toward God. What is Dostoevski's attitude? (II)

Desiderius Erasmus: *In Praise of Folly;* Edmund Spenser: *The Faerie Queene*

HUMAN PERFECTIBILITY: ERASMUS AND SPENSER

Examine In Praise of Folly *and* The Faerie Queene, *Book VI. Compare and contrast the authors' views on the possibility of human perfectibility.*

What internal and external factors oppose perfection? According to either author, is everyone capable of achieving perfection? (II)

Gustave Flaubert: *Madame Bovary*

ISOLATION IN *Madame Bovary*

Discuss the theme of isolation in Flaubert's novel.

What techniques does Flaubert use to present his theme? (II)

André Gide: *The Counterfeiters, Journal of "The Counterfeiters"*

THE NARRATIVE TECHNIQUE OF *The Counterfeiters*

A discussion of the various narrative devices in The Counterfeiters *and the effect that they produce on the reader.*

Separate the different strands of the narrative: the various speakers, the notebooks, etc. How many different narrators are there, and who are they? Is any of them Gide? The notebooks are for a novel entitled "The Counterfeiters"; how does this affect our view of the book? How does the book violate novelistic tradition? Are we inside or outside the book? (You could take into account Gide's *Journal of "The Counterfeiters"* in answering the latter questions.) (III)

Johann Wolfgang von Goethe: *Faust*

THE REDEMPTION OF FAUST

Why is Faust redeemed?

Discuss what Faust does to avoid damnation. Pay special attention to the terms of the pact. Is grace involved? Who confers it? (I)

Johann Wolfgang von Goethe: *Faust*

THE ROLE OF MEPHISTOPHELES IN *Faust*

Is Mephistopheles a villain? a tragic hero? Or does he play some other part?

A careful reading of the text. The play is so long that one must be alert to changes in his role during the play; note also that Mephistopheles adopts certain roles as part of larger roles. (II)

Heinrich Heine: "Im wunderschönen Monat Mai," "Du bist wie eine Blume"

PATTERNS OF IMAGERY IN TWO POEMS OF HEINE

A study of Heine's image patterns.

Compare and contrast the two poems. Pay special attention to the manner in which Heine develops his images. What kind of pattern is he using and why? (II)

Henrik Ibsen: *The Enemy of the People*

The Enemy of the People

A discussion of Ibsen's play.

It is evident that Ibsen's title is ironic, that the central character is not an "enemy of the people." Who is the real enemy of the people? How did you reach this conclusion? (II)

Henrik Ibsen: *Rosmersholm;* August Strindberg: *The Father*

PSYCHIC MURDER IN *Rosmersholm* AND *The Father*

An investigation of the idea of psychic murder and its dramatization in these two plays.

For Strindberg, the concept of psychic murder solved the problem of a dramatic form for Naturalism. He felt that if psychic murder were used as a major plot element it would be easy to produce a naturalistic drama. Evaluate how the idea is used in these two texts, and decide whether or not the result is a naturalistic drama in each case. (III)

Henrik Ibsen, George Bernard Shaw: plays

IBSEN AND SHAW: THE DEMISE OF A CLASSICAL TRADITION

Are Ibsen and Shaw really the last of the classical dramatists writing in the Germanic languages?

Determine the extent of the break made by succeeding authors with the tradition of Ibsen and Shaw. Are Ibsen and Shaw in the mainstream of tradition? To what extent do they break with accepted forms?   (II)

Eugène Ionesco: *Rhinoceros, Tueur sans Gages*

THE PROBLEM OF BERENGER

What is the significance of Ionesco's continuing character Berenger?

Compare and contrast the works in which Berenger appears. Consider the problem of chronology. Is Berenger the same character? If so, why did the killer not kill him?   (II)

Franz Kafka: novels and short stories

KAFKA'S REALITY

A study of reality in the work of Kafka.

Consider Kafka's settings. The pictures he draws show extreme distortions. Why? What does he achieve? What is the philosophical basis for this? How effective is it?   (II)

Sören Kierkegaard: *Repetition, Either/Or, Fear and Trembling, The Concluding Unscientific Postscript;*
Samuel Beckett, Eugene Ionesco: plays

KIERKEGAARD AND THE THEATRE OF THE ABSURD

An analysis of his influence on Absurdist work.

Kierkegaard's thought should be analyzed to discover which of his ideas are susceptible of dramatic use or exposition. Typical Absurdist works should then be investigated with these ideas in mind. Particular attention should be paid to the concept of Repetition.   (III)

Le Conte de Lautréamont: *Songs of Maldoror;* Arthur Rimbaud: poetry

A COMPARISON OF RIMBAUD AND LAUTRÉAMONT

Compare and contrast the styles of these two poets.

Analyze theme, style, and techniques of a few selected works of these poets.   (III)

Federico Garcia Lorca: "The Old Lizard," "The Lizard Is Crying"

LORCA'S USE OF IMAGES

A study of the two poems "The Old Lizard" and "The Lizard Is Crying."

How does Lorca's choice of images affect our feelings in these poems? Are they necessarily symbolic or do they exist for their own sake (cf. the images of the sky and the sun in "The Lizard Is Crying")? Why are these poems so moving? Would you say that Lorca uses images to appeal to the intellect or to less conscious responses?

(II)

Martin Luther: hymns

THE HYMNS OF MARTIN LUTHER

A critical evaluation of Luther's hymns, considered as poetry.

Examine the form and structure of each poem. Consider such topics as the coherence of structure

with theme, power and depth of images, patterns.
Remember that these hymns are the initial steps
in the composition of a liturgy. How successful
are they?   (II)

Thomas Mann: *The Magic Mountain*

PAINFUL, MYSTERIOUS, AND FERTILE

A study of Hans Castorp as the archetypal quester.

What is Castorp seeking? Does he find it? How
does he proceed? What makes him archetypal?
                                                             (III)

Thomas Mann: *Buddenbrooks*

THE PROGRESSION OF THE GENERATIONS IN
    Buddenbrooks

*A discussion of the development of the Budden-
brooks from generation to generation.*

What differentiates the members of the family in
each generation? How does their character
change? What different forces act on them? How
does their approach to the world change? How
and why does the family reach its final decline?
                                                             (II)

Molière: *That Scoundrel Scapin;* Plautus: *Formio*

THE ROLE OF THE SERVANT IN COMEDY

*Discuss the role of the servant in comedy. What
are some of his universal characteristics?*

How is the servant generally presented?   (I)

Michel de Montaigne: *The Apology for Raymond Sabonde;*
William Shakespeare: *Hamlet*

The Apology for Raymond Sabonde AND *Hamlet*

How is Montaigne's work related in spirit to Shakespeare's?

Characterize the wisdom of the essay and of the character Hamlet and relate the two.   (III)

Friedrich Nietzsche: *Thus Spoke Zarathustra;*
Ralph Waldo Emerson: essays

NIETZSCHE ON EMERSON

Write a reflection from a Nietzschean point of view on the philosophical doctrine of Emerson.

How would Nietzsche view such essential concepts of Emerson as those of morality and individualism?   (III)

François Rabelais: *Gargantua;*
Giovanni Boccaccio: *The Decameron*

HUMOR IN RABELAIS AND BOCCACCIO

Compare the types of humor and the humorous devices in these two works.

Why does each author use humor? What types of humor does each employ?   (II)

Rainer Maria Rilke: *Collected Works*

A MAN AND HIS GOD

A study of the religious development of Rainer Maria Rilke.

Consider typical works from various moments in Rilke's life. Examine the religious position expressed, if any. How does this develop? Why?

(II)

Stendahl: *The Red and the Black, The Charterhouse of Parma*

ROMANTICISM AND REALISM IN STENDAHL

Discuss the combination of styles in Stendahl's work. What purpose does it serve?

What characteristics of each style does Stendahl employ? Do you think he is more of a realist or a romantic? Why?   (II)

Stendahl: *The Charterhouse of Parma*

A COMPARISON OF CLÉLIA AND LA SANSSÉVÉRINA

Analyze the characters of these two heroines.

What are the motives of these two women? What function does each one serve? How is each presented?   (II)

August Strindberg: *A Dream Play*

STRINDBERG ON *A Dream Play*

"On a flimsy foundation of actual happening, imagination spins and weaves in new patterns: an inter-mingling of remembrances, experiences, whims, fancies, ideas, fantastic absurdities and improvisation, and original inventions of the mind. . . . There is, however, one single-minded consciousness that exercises a dominance over the character's: the dreamer's."

Does the playwright succeed in his intention, and does his comment help towards an understanding of the play?   (II)

August Strindberg: *A Dream Play;*
Eugene O'Neill: *The Emperor Jones;*
Georg Kaiser: *Alkibiades Saved*

DISTORTION IN EXPRESSIONISM

One of the chief attributes of expressionism is distortion—visual, verbal, and emotional.

Discuss this concept. Determine whether or not distortion furthers the intent of the dramatist.

                                              (II)

Leo Tolstoi: *Anna Karenina*

RUSSIAN SOCIETY IN THE NINETEENTH CENTURY

A portrayal of Russian society in Anna Karenina.

How does Tolstoy portray Russian society in *Anna Karenina?* What techniques does he use? Does he refer to all classes in Russia at that time? How? What is his own opinion? Does he prefigure the Russian Revolution?   (II)

François Voltaire: *Zadig, Candide*

A COMPARISON OF *Zadig* AND *Candide*

A study of the change in Voltaire's philosophy as presented in Zadig *and* Candide.

These two works were written during two different periods of Voltaire's life, and suggest changes in his philosophy. What are these changes, and how does he present them?   (II)

MISCELLANEOUS TOPICS

Jean Anouilh: *Ardèle*

IRONY IN *Ardèle*

Anouilh's Ardèle *is an almost totally ironic play, in which everything undergoes some sort of deflation. What is the final message of the play?*

Examine the play carefully for inversions of expected values and expected behavior. How does Anouilh achieve the irony in this play, and what is the final effect on the reader?   (II)

Pierre de Beaumarchais: *The Marriage of Figaro*

SOCIAL COMMENT IN BEAUMARCHAIS

What was Beaumarchais' attitude toward eighteenth-century French society?

Discuss Beaumarchais' social criticism in *The Marriage of Figaro*. What is so extraordinary about the hero of this play? In what way does the play prefigure the Revolution?   (II)

Thomas More: *Utopia;*
Samuel Butler: *Erewhon;*
George Orwell: *1984;*
Aldous Huxley: *Brave New World;*
Robert Heinlein: *Beyond This Horizon;*
Isaac Asimov: *The Foundation Trilogy*

SCIENCE FICTION AND THE UTOPIAN NOVEL

An investigation of the differences between science fiction and the Utopian novel.

Compare and contrast the two forms. Show how

differences in style and form support intended differences in theme.   (I)

Sean O'Casey: *The Plough and the Stars*

STAGE DEVICES AND DRAMATIC CONTENT: *The Plough and the Stars*

What is the relationship between the dramatic devices employed in the play and the themes expressed by the play? Where are stage devices symbolic or emblematic of the things O'Casey is talking about?

Note the use of various stage devices—for instance, the frequent intrusion of fire and the use made of doors and windows—and attempt to show how these devices bear on the message of the play and help to present it to us.   (II)

Sinclair Lewis: *Elmer Gantry, Main Street;* Charles Dickens: *Hard Times;* Honoré de Balzac: *Père Goriot;* Truman Capote: *In Cold Blood*

JOURNALISM AND FICTION

When novelists use a journalistic style in an attempt to expose a specific evil in their society, does the total artistic effect of the work suffer?

Can a good journalist be a good novelist?   (II)

William Congreve: *The Way of the World;* Richard Sheridan: *The Rivals;* Ben Jonson: *The Alchemist;* Oliver Goldsmith: *She Stoops to Conquer*

WIT AND HUMOR

What is the difference between wit and humor?

Consider the Restoration playwrights. What did they mean by wit? Does it subsume humor? Does

humor subsume wit? What is their relationship?
(III)

Alexander Pope, Samuel Johnson, Laurence Sterne: appropriate works

THE EVOLUTION OF THE PUN

Contrast the use of the pun in eighteenth-century English literature with its use today.

We now use the pun for comic purposes, to emphasize the ultimate separation of objects. Show how these three eighteenth-century authors used the pun to a different purpose.   (III)

Edmund Burke: *An Inquiry into the Sublime and the Beautiful;* Longinus: *On the Sublime*

WHAT IS THE SUBLIME?

With the help of literary critics, try to derive a definition of "sublime."

Consider the discussions on this topic by Burke and Longinus. *King Lear* and *Paradise Lost* are generally considered examples of the sublime. Why? Can you think of a twentieth-century work that might be called sublime?   (III)

Erich Maria Remarque: *All Quiet on the Western Front;* Norman Mailer: *The Naked and the Dead;* Rupert Brooke: poems; Jean Anouilh: *Antigone;* Aristophanes: *Lysistrata*

WAR AND LITERATURE

A study of the effect of warfare on literature.

Compare and contrast works written during or after a major war. Note the contrast in quality between works written during and works written after. Why?   (II)

Francis Bacon, William Shakespeare, John Milton: works

BACON TO SHAKESPEARE ON MILTON

Write a letter from Bacon to the Bard discussing Milton.

Determine Bacon's personality from his work. Evaluate his reaction to Milton's work, and express his reaction as Bacon would when addressing Shakespeare.   (II)

Christopher Marlowe: *Doctor Faustus;* Samuel Beckett: *Waiting for Godot*

TIME IN *Doctor Faustus* AND *Waiting for Godot*

What is the significance and function of time in each play? Compare and contrast the two conceptions of time.

How is time related to the world in which the characters live? How do they come to terms with time in each play?   (II)

St. Paul: Epistles; St. Augustine: *Confessions*

CHRISTIAN LOVE IN THE LETTERS OF ST. PAUL AND THE *Confessions* OF ST. AUGUSTINE

Compare and contrast the ideas of love in these works.

How do the differences in the conception of Christian love reflect differing views on man and God?   (III)

William Shakespeare: *King Lear;* Jonathan Swift: *Gulliver's Travels;* Nathaniel Hawthorne: *The Scarlet Letter*

"THE FALL OF MAN STANDS A LIE BEFORE BEETHOVEN, A TRUTH BEFORE HITLER"

A study of what various authors would have thought about this quotation from Gregory Corso.

Consider the attitude of Shakespeare, Swift, and Hawthorne toward this line. How would they interpret it? Would they approve?   (II)

Alfred Noyes: "The Highwayman"; Francis Child: *The English and Scottish Popular Ballad;* **Rudyard Kipling: appropriate works**

THE BALLAD IN THE NINETEENTH CENTURY

An investigation of the popularity of the ballad in nineteenth-century England.

Look for common themes among the poets using the ballad form. Why was its popularity so great, and so short-lived? Develop a theory that indicates why only the ballad could have served the need it did, whatever that was?   (III)

Aristotle: *Poetics;* **Sophocles:** *Oedipus Rex;* **Eugene O'Neill:** *Mourning Becomes Electra;* **Arthur Miller:** *Death of a Salesman;* **Tennessee Williams:** *A Streetcar Named Desire*

TRAGEDY IN THE TWENTIETH CENTURY

Is it possible to write a tragedy in the twentieth century?

Consider the nature of tragedy. Compare the theory of tragedy as practiced by the ancients with what passes for tragedy today. Is the ancient theory complete? Decide if the texts you consider are or are not tragedies.   (II)

Jean Anouilh: *Ardèle;* **Samuel Beckett:** *Waiting for Godot;* **William Alfred:** *Hogan's Goat;* **Anton Chekhov:** *Three Sisters;* **Federico Garcia Lorca:** *The House of Bernarda Alba*

THE INVISIBLE CHARACTER IN MODERN DRAMA

How are characters who never appear on stage utilized in recent drama? How do different authors treat them?

How important are these invisible characters? If they are important, why do they not come on stage? What is the use of their never appearing?

(II)

Francis Child: *The English and Scottish Popular Ballad*

THE BEAUTY OF THE BALLAD

A study of form and structure in the English ballad.

The English ballad has a long history and has taken many forms. The problem is to establish categories and select typical works of each category. Justify your choices. Develop a theory to account for your categories and their relationships.

(I)

Herman Melville: *Moby Dick;* Nathaniel Hawthorne: *The Scarlet Letter*

THE DEMOCRATIZATION OF TRAGEDY: HAWTHORNE AND MELVILLE

Show how Hawthorne and Melville reduced the classical concept of tragedy of great men to the tragedy of the human soul caught in darkness.

Compare the characters of Ahab and Dimmesdale with a classical hero. In what way do the causes of their doom differ? How does these two authors' relation of tragedy to interior rather than exterior forces open the way for a new conception of tragedy in American literature?

(II)

Jack Kerouac: *On the Road, The Dharma Bums, Doctor Sax;* **Lawrence Ferlinghetti:** *HER*

THE STRUCTURE OF THE BEAT NOVEL

An investigation of the coherence of the Beat novel as a work of art.

Examine the structure of typical Beat novels in light of its relevance to theme, etc. Special attention should be paid to the problem of coherence in these texts.   (III)

T. S. Eliot: *Tradition and the Individual Talent,* **poetry**

WHAT IS THE OBJECTIVE CORRELATIVE?

A discussion of T. S. Eliot's term "objective correlative" and a definition of what it means to you.

Read Eliot's essay *Tradition and the Individual Talent* and any others that you wish to read. Attempt a definition of "objective correlative" and look for it in his poetry and that of other authors. How does the objective correlative relate to his whole view of literature?   (II)

Henry Fielding, Samuel Richardson, Tobias Smollett, Daniel Defoe: novels

NARRATIVE TECHNIQUE IN THE EIGHTEENTH CENTURY

Compare the three basic eighteenth-century narrative techniques—epistolary style, first-person memoir style, and third-person narration.

In each instance, discuss the potentiality for character development, "realistic" narration of events, and immediacy of action.   (III)

Snorri Sturluson: *Prose Edda; Heimskringla; Njal's Saga; Gunnlaug's Saga*

THE ICELANDIC SAGAS

A study of the Icelandic sagas.

Analysis and tabulation of the characteristics of the Icelandic sagas. (II)

D. H. Lawrence: *St. Mawr;* T. S. Eliot: *The Waste Land*

St. Mawr AND *The Waste Land*

A comparison of D. H. Lawrence's St. Mawr *with Eliot's poem.*

Both of these works are comprehensive statements about the modern world. How are they similar in theme and technique? How does each author see the present day? Does either of them see a way out of the present condition? How do they differ? (III)

William Wycherly: *The Country Wife*

The Country Wife

An attempt to clarify Wycherly's drama.

Is this play really a comedy? Examine the ending and determine if Horner's fate is appropriate to his role as a comic hero. What does Wycherly intend? Why is this play great? (III)

Wilfred Owen: war poetry

WILFRED OWEN—STYLE AND EXPERIENCE

How does the style of Owen's poetry reflect the horror of war?

Relate the peculiarities of Owen's poetics and imagery to his experience.   (II)

Benedetto Croce: *The Concept of History as Subsumed by Art*

CAN HISTORY BE CONSIDERED ART?

A study of Croce's great essay.

Consider and debate Croce's arguments. Investigate the validity of his examples. Raise opposing examples.   (III)

Gregory Corso: *A Happy Birthday of Death;* Lawrence Ferlinghetti: *A Coney Island of the Mind;* Allen Ginsberg: *Howl*

THE BEAT USE OF HUMOR

An exploration of the use of humor as a literary device by the Beat poets.

A detailed textual examination of typical Beat texts. This study should reveal how the poets have employed humor to support and enhance their work.   (II)

Jean Racine: *Phèdre;* Jean Anouilh: *Antigone;* Albert Camus: *The Myth of Sisyphus*

THE CONTINUANCE OF THE CLASSICAL TRADITION IN FRENCH LITERATURE

Demonstrate the continuance of the classical influence upon French literature through the present day.

Choose several works from various periods and analyze the authors' use of classical subject matter. How are the works adapted to their time? (I)

Antonin Artaud: *The Theatre and Its Double;* Albert Camus: *Caligula, The Rebel;* Eugène Ionesco: *Amédée, The Lesson;* Alfred Jarry: *Ubu Roi*

'PATAPHYSICS IN RELATION TO THE PHILOSOPHY OF MODERN DRAMA

In what way does the 'pataphysical movement relate to the Cruel and the Absurd?

Artaud's *The Theatre and Its Double* and Camus' *The Rebel* present philosophical bases for much modern theater: Artaud calling for the anarchic, the visceral, the sensational, and Camus defending the interpersonal, the idiosyncratic, the "absurd." However, they were both foreshadowed by Jarry in *Ubu Roi*, which embodies many of their concepts.   (I)

John Webster: *The White Devil, The Duchess of Malfi;* Cyril Tourneur: *The Atheists' Tragedy, The Avenger's Tragedy;* William Shakespeare: *Hamlet*

BLOOD, DEATH AND THE PEN

A study of the characteristics of the tragedy of blood.

(Approach with extreme caution.) Compare and contrast the texts, looking for common elements. Try to distinguish the significant from the merely relevant. What is the function of morality in these plays? How is morality conceived of? Are they really tragedy or are they melodrama as high art?   (III)

Kenneth Rexroth: *100 Poems from the Chinese, 100 Poems from the Japanese*

POETRY OF CHINA AND JAPAN

A comparison of Chinese and Japanese poetry.

How does the poetry of China and Japan differ in style and technique? Do the poets' intentions seem to be the same? In what way are they similar? Do they concentrate on the same subjects? What ideas of form seem to govern each type of poetry? (II)

Kenneth Rexroth: *100 Poems from the Japanese*

THE TECHNIQUE OF JAPANESE POETRY

A discussion of what effects Japanese poetry achieves, and how it does so.

What effects do you think the poets intended to achieve in writing their poems? Do they have the same intentions as Western poets? What areas of poetic expression do they concentrate on? What are the main characteristics of the style? How does Japanese poetry compare with modern Western poetry (particularly Imagist poetry)? (II)

Charles Dickens: *Great Expectations;* **John Knowles:** *A Separate Peace*

THE *Bildungsroman* IN TWO CENTURIES

A comparison of Great Expectations *and* A Separate Peace.

The *Bildungsroman,* or novel of growing up, is a frequently used form in English literature. Compare the ways in which these two works treat the story of a boy attaining adulthood. How do they differ in technique? Do they concentrate on different areas of the subject? How has the passing of a century affected the form? (II)

[Anonymous]: *The Second Shepherd's Play; Everyman*

MYSTERY AND MORALITY PLAYS ON THE MODERN STAGE

Would the mystery and morality plays be accepted on the stage today, even though they are so unlike modern drama? If so, why?

Examine the concepts presented in these plays. Do you think that modern audiences would respond to these works?   (II)

John Keats: letters and poems

WHAT IS NEGATIVE CAPABILITY?

A discussion of Keats' famous term "negative capability" and what it means to you.

Read Keats' letter on "negative capability" and attempt to assess what he means by his definition of it. Look for evidence of negative capability in his own poetry and attempt to relate it to other statements he makes about poetry in his letters.   (II)

Allen Ginsberg: *Howl, Kaddish;* Gregory Corso: poems; Lawrence Ferlinghetti: poems; Jack Kerouac: *On the Road;* Michael McClure: *A New Book: A Book of Torture*

WHAT IS THE BEAT?

An investigation of the basic tenets of the Beat school.

An examination of the theme and content of Beat texts.   (II)

Antonin Artaud: *The Theatre and Its Double;*
Peter Weiss: *Marat/Sade;* **Peter Schaffer:**
The Royal Hunt of the Sun

WHAT IS THE THEATRE OF CRUELTY?

A discussion of the Theatre of Cruelty.

Consider the theory and practice of the Theatre of
Cruelty. What distinguishes it from other dramatic literature—in theory and in practice? Is it
an improvement over the standard theatre? Evaluate the potential of this form.   (II)

Anthony Trollope: *Barchester Towers*

THE PRESENCE OF THE AUTHOR IN *Barchester
Towers*

*Discuss the extent and affect of the author's voice
and opinions in the novel.*

Why does the author intrude his tone and judgments into the course of the narrative? How does
this affect the representation of reality?   (II)

John Hersey: *Hiroshima*

MODERN HISTORY AS MODERN LITERATURE: JOHN
HERSEY

*Discuss the literary value of the dramatization of
actual events as exemplified in John Hersey's*
Hiroshima.

How does such a presentation as *Hiroshima* differ
from a straightforward relation of the historic
facts? To what extent is the author's presence and
point of view made clear? You may wish to relate this discussion to the controversial discussion
of the "nonfiction novel."   (II)

Thomas Wyatt; Henry Howard, Earl of Surrey; Sir Phillip Sidney; William Shakespeare; Michael Drayton: sonnets

THE EVOLUTION OF THE ELIZABETHAN SONNET

Discuss the changes of form and subject matter in the English sonnet from its introduction by Thomas Wyatt through the sonnet cycle of Michael Drayton.

Consider changes in rhyme, scheme, and changes in the function of metaphor. What are the effects of these changes upon the general movement of the individual poem? Is there consistency of subject matter? (I)

Knut Hamsun: *Pan, Hunger;* Pär Lagerkvist: *The Dwarf, The Sibyl*

THE MODERN SCANDINAVIAN NOVEL

An analysis of the modern Scandinavian novel.

Consider theme, style, and other characteristics of these modern Scandinavian novels. (II)

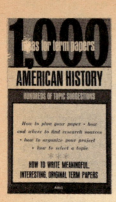

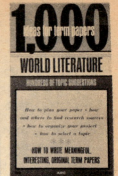